How to Improve Your Life by Applying Eternal Laws

Twenty-Six Universal Laws Plus How Universal and God's Eternal Laws Are Intertwined within the Scriptures for our Benefit and Blessings

Sonja Ervin

ISBN 978-1-64003-651-2 (Paperback)
ISBN 978-1-64003-652-9 (Digital)

Covenant Books, Inc.
11661 Hwy 707
Murrells Inlet, SC 29576
www.covenantbooks.com

Contents

Acknowledgments

There is so much to acknowledge or be grateful for that I'm not sure where to begin.

Where in your life do you start saying thank you for the experiences you gain that develops wisdom and, hopefully, a sense of truth? Is it when you are a young child soaking in values and behaviors or when you have sort of figured life out in your midyears or when you are a bit older and looking back at your bucket of trials, truths, and trusts? Or perhaps after you understand your purpose and realized how great and valuable your life is—being a son or daughter of a God who makes each of us amazing and wonderful.

Or I could start with my gratitude for having a laptop that I can spill myself out on, and it remembers everything that I write, especially if I save it! Or my home with a mountain looming up into the sky as I admire it from my window, giving me joy and amazement at its grandeur, truly a blessing from God's mighty creations.

But I think I will start with people. All the family, friends, and strangers that have entered and touched my learning and love. People that have made me happy and gave me the opportunity to wrap my life around and love. My parents, my brothers and sister, my husband and dear children and grandchildren. I thank the many individuals that have made this book possible, and I thank the many that this book will inspire for good.

At the top of the list, however, is a big massive thank-you to God and the inspiration of the Holy Ghost in putting down what best to say in my own voice. Words that come from my heart that I pray will touch yours.

I would like to dedicate this book to all those who desire happiness by following the Laws that produce blessings. But more importantly, to my precious husband who supported me all along the way and to my wonderful children—I will always love and be grateful for the opportunity to be your mother.

Photo via VisualHunt

For the commandment is a lamp;
and the law is light; and reproofs of
instruction are the way of life.

—Proverbs 6:23

Introduction

It seems through study and observation of my life, that laws played—and still do—a major part on how organized and fulfilled my life has established itself thus far in my existence. Without really realizing it or understanding it, all the actions and decisions that have formed my life up to this point have actually been in accordance to how I have obeyed natural laws, Laws of God, and Laws of Man.

I have been aware of some natural, Universal Laws and have even purchased many books on the subject and have lightly read through them, but I never really *got* the concept of such laws until recently. I guess back then I was "touched" or "introduced" to the amazement of such laws, but never really took them to heart until now. I'm not sure why it is "now" that I have jumped in with both feet, so to speak, but I have found them fascinating and truly eternal.

Understanding and applying Universal Laws into my day-to-day has turned my life around to a much more wondrous and fulfilling adventure indeed! The Law of Cause and Effect, the Law of Attraction, the Law of Sacrifice, the Law of Gratitude, to name just a few. When they are recognized and practiced, they can really waken an individual up to the possibilities of establishing one's pure potential and then using that purpose to enlighten the surrounding world. What a great movement that would be!

And then I realized that God utilizes eternal Laws as well to work and help us (his children on earth) to live with purpose and blessings. Laws, when obeyed, will bring us greater joy and happiness and draw us closer to our inner spirit and soul. Even our Lord and Savior, Jesus Christ, came to earth to fulfill the eternal law of Justice. When mistakes and sins or shortcoming are performed that breaks the law, then someone, if it's not the guilty individual, has to pay the price and atone for them. Because of Christ's great love for us, he chose to suffer and make restitution—if we choose to let him.

So what are the Universal Laws and how do they relate to the scriptures? How can we use them in our lives to further our potential, our purpose, our happiness, and our joy? This book has been researched and written for that very reason—to bring us all to a greater understanding of what some of nature's Universal Laws are and how we can use them in our daily lives to have a much wealthier, joyous, earthly life. Also, to realize that our Father works in an organized manner using eternal laws as well to form the existence of nature and man (all God's children on earth) and how he has given us the choice to obey and return to him by applying into our lives eternally established Universal Laws.

There is a scripture that has always captured my attention. It reads,

There is a law, irrevocably decreed in heaven before the foundations of this world, upon which all blessings, are predicated—And when we obtain any blessing from God, it is by obedience to that law upon which it is predicated. (D&C 130:20–21)

In addition to this scripture, there is written another which says, "For all who will have a blessing at my hands shall abide the law which was appointed for that blessing, and the conditions whereof, as were instituted from before the foundation of the world" (D&C 132:5). Clearly and precisely; laws are a part of mortality, and delightful blessings are a condition of obedience.

What are these laws? What are the blessings? Which law do I need to live to receive which blessing? I hope this book brings us to more enlightenment and understanding of the wonder of God's laws and the blessings it brings into our lives when we obey. For God said, "I, the Lord, am bound when ye do what I say; but when ye do not what I say, ye have not promise" (D&C 82:10). Our obedience to natural laws brings us a guarantee of blessings and tender mercies if we keep our part of the arrangement. The Lord will not change his mind either. "For I am the Lord, I change not; . . ." (3 Nephi 24:6).

I have found this project quite interesting, and I hope you do too. Here is to all of us in learning and obeying natural laws to improve our lives, our hopes, and our dreams. And here is to our most creative Father above in giving us laws so we can exist in our happiest state—for he knows all things and knows all of us.

As D&C 88:41 proclaims,

He comprehendeth all things, and all things are before him, and all things are round about him; and he is above all things, and in all things, and is through all things, and is round about all things; and all things are by him, and of him, even God, forever and ever.

Chapter 1

What is the Deal with Laws Anyway?

Why are laws necessary?
Why are they important to our happiness?

It seems that we cannot exist without laws. The earth was created using the eternal natural laws of manipulating elements to form an earth and galaxy that our world revolves in. God used Universal Laws to generate a place that emanates incredible beauty and wonder, a place that oozes in abundance and order.

So it makes sense that eternal laws have always existed for nothing can be created or formed into being without using established rules to do so. One cannot grow a simple flower without the need for the Universal Law of Germination or the Law of Harvest—to place the seed into nutrient-rich soil, to take root downward, and then to rise up heavenward and burst into blossom. How could that happen without certain natural laws in place to be able to guide the seed of what to do? Water, sun, good soil, capable seed equal a developed plant. It happens—by law.

Of course there are different kinds of laws that guide our lives. Eternal Laws-Universal Laws and Laws of God-

and Man-Made Laws. The first have always been. They are how we and our universe came to be, they have always been and they will always exist—unchangeable and everlasting. Eternal, natural laws gives light and life to everything, and even God uses these laws. In D&C 88:13, it states, "The light which is in all things, which giveth life to all things, which is the law by which all things are governed, even the power of God who sitteth upon his throne, who is in the bosom of eternity, who is in the midst of all things."

Other laws on earth have become into being, either temporarily or through necessity for peace and order for humans to dwell together without chaos and for freedom. Man-made laws may be different from place to place or from country to country, formed for the betterment of the society that lives there. Government can change laws to fit the need of its society or how the jurisdiction develops or how it can be modified from year to year. Man can tweak laws or establish new ones by popular vote even if a minority of citizens do not support them. They still become law for the masses to obey and form their lives around.

Mosiah explains this electoral process by voice of the people when he teaches,

Therefore, choose you by the voice of this people, judges, that ye may be judged according to the laws which have been given you by our fathers, which are correct, and which were given them by the hand of the Lord.

Now it is not common that the voice of the people desireth anything contrary to that which is right; but it is common for the lesser part of the people to desire that which is not right; therefore this shall ye observe and make it your law—to do your business by the voice of the people.

And if the time comes that the voice of the people doth choose iniquity, then is the time that the judgments of God will come upon you; yea, then is the time he will visit you with great destruction even as he has hitherto visited this land.

And now if ye have judges, and they do not judge you according to the law which has been given, ye can cause that they may be judged of a higher judge.

If your higher judges do no judge righteous judgments, ye shall cause that a small number of your lower judges should be gathered together, and they shall judge your higher judges, according to the voice of the people. (Mosiah 29:25–29)

Our past beloved leader, Prophet Joseph Smith, anchored the churches beliefs down when the 13 Articles of Faith, number 12 states, "We believe in being subject to kings, presidents, rulers, and magistrates, in obeying, honoring, and sustaining the law" (Pearl of Great Price). This states our beliefs quite bluntly in how we should be behaving in relevance to our man-made laws.

Our forefathers—with pen in hand—tediously and tirelessly formed constitutions that were meant for the betterment of mankind and for everyone's freedoms for such causes as the right to be educated, to believe what we want, to form families, to work and to speak. Surely, these man-made laws are extremely important so people can exist together through differences of opinion and thoughts of what is best for their development, for the good of themselves, their families, and others. Hopefully, these are the kinds of man-made laws that will not change, but lesser laws come and go that were relevant for the time but became ridiculous as time went on—for instance, not being able to play bingo longer than five hours at a time or to more serious ones like voting rights for women. The point is that man-made laws change or can be changed, and Universal, eternal laws do not.

Laws give us order and bring us blessings when obeyed. They also give us instruction on how to meet our divine potential as children of God. When we understand and study Universal Laws or natural laws and Laws of God through the scriptures, that our eyes are open to the possibilities of great happiness in fulfilling ourselves and assisting others to do the same. King Benjamin in Mosiah 2:41 beautifully proclaimed,

> And moreover, I would desire that ye should consider on the blessed and happy state of those that keep the commandments of God, For behold, they are blessed in all things, both temporal and spiritual; and if they hold out faithful to the end they are received into heaven, that thereby they may dwell with God in a state of never-ending happiness. O remember, remember that these things are true; for the Lord God hath spoken it.

"For the commandment like unto is a lamp; and the law is light; and reproofs of instruction are the way of life" (Prov. 6:23). We all appreciate a warm light in a dark room or a flickering beacon of safety that a campfire grounds us to, while surrounded by trees blanketed by night's veil. Eternal Laws of God and righteous laws of man define the course we can follow for peace, joy, and safety. These laws are divine. They were established before the foundation of the world was designed and created. As an informative scripture relates, "For all who will have a blessing at my hands shall abide the law which was appointed for that blessing, and the conditions thereof, as were instituted from before the foundation of the world" (D&C 132:5).

Now some people think that laws are restrictive and binding to their freedom, whereas the opposite is the case. Laws *give* us freedom. They do not chain us down like the disobedience of following God's laws would. Most people can understand that when taking illegal drugs, for example. It coils our bodies in health-damaging habits and diminishes our control of mind and body, whereas, if obedience to sustain from habitual substances were obeyed, then freedom would be our existence, and the ability to choose would be at our unhampered discretion.

Even though obedience to laws will bring us profound blessings, we still have the ability within ourselves to choice to follow the established law or not. Even the ability to make a choice ourselves is a law. There is no forcing, but we still reap the consequences of our actions, be it right to follow the laws and receive prescribed blessing or accumulate disappointments and heartaches through disobedience. This is not a new concept. Choices started from our beginning on earth from Adam and Eve. {1} Even they had decisions to make between one thing or another. Each had its consequences, but selecting the choice best for human-kind was needed and necessary. The natural Law of Cause and Effect fits within this picture.

The verse in 2 Nephi 10:23 lifts up our spirits with the right to make choices for ourselves. It says, "Therefore, cheer up your hearts, and remember that ye are free to act for yourselves—to choose the way of everlasting death or the way of eternal life." Thus, by following the laws of God and nature, it gives us great joy, peace, and eternal life. God created and followed eternal laws. They are the perfect law of liberty (James 1:25).

The Gospel is a great system of laws, which laws are simply eternal principles by which our Father in heaven desires to save mankind, his sons and his daughters. Not only to save them but also to share it with them all that the Father has—associations with those we love, honor, power, glory, dominions, even exaltation.{2} It makes no differ-ence if you obey a law of nature, a law of God, or a law of man or not. It doesn't change the fact that the law is the law, and it's not going anywhere or changing, and the con-sequences of not following a law or reaping blessings from a law. It's just the way it is. You cannot avoid or pretend a law isn't there or it doesn't concern you or that you can just get around it. Eternal laws are "written in stone"—so to speak—so just live them and be blessed by them! In D&C 88:34, it plainly states, "And again, verily I say unto you, that which is governed by law is also preserved by law and perfected and sanctified by the same." An eternal law is saved by itself.

Then there is the fact that if there is a law, there is punishment if disobeyed, and if there is no law, how can anyone sin? "Now, how could a man repent except he should sin? How could he sin if there was no law? How could there be a law save there was a punishment?" (Alma 42:17). Laws and consequences go together. There are either blessings from following and living the laws or a person reaps not—so desired consequences for choosing not to obey them. One cannot be without the other. This arrangement also follows the Law of Polarity or Opposites—black/white, law/outcome, happy/sad, and so forth.

Understanding how laws operate in your life is crucial. They are perfect. No debate or discussion about natural, eternal laws. They don't change. You don't have to check in on them now and then to see if they are different from yesterday's laws. If you follow the law the way it states, the outcome will always happen and manifest itself—guarantied!

For example, 2 Nephi 1:20 definitely lays it on the line when it says, "Inasmuch as ye shall keep my commandments ye shall prosper in the land; but inasmuch as ye will not keep my commandments ye shall be cut off from my presence." If you do this, then this will be your reward, but if you don't do this, then this negatively happens! And again D&C 82:10, "I, the Lord, am bound when ye do what I say; but when ye do not what I say, ye have no promise." Most concerned parent says this same scenario to their own children—"When you make your bed, then you can go outside and play." Or, "You can use the car after you wash it." The natural law of cause and effect fits into this nicely. God works with laws. We receive blessings when we obey laws.

Elder Bruce R. McConkie said,

> All things are governed by law; nothing is
> exempt. In the eternal perspective there is no
> such thing as chance; in the divine economy
> the same in varying result always flows
> from the same cause. These principles are
> immutable, eternal, everlasting; they apply
> to all things both temporal and spiritual . . .
> There is no whim, chance, or caprice in the
> operation of gospel law. Divine blessings
> always result from obedience to the law upon
> which their receipt is predicated . . . Once a
> law has been ordained, it thereafter operates
> automatically; that is, whenever there is
> compliance with its terms and conditions, the
> promised (blessings) accrue . . . {3} [3AR]

As you can see, our lives are guided by laws, if we agree
with them or not. Laws make it possible to receive blessings
and instruction for the betterment of ourselves, our family, and our neighborhood. God's laws are eternal. Natural
Universal Laws are never changing. The following chapter
discusses the difference as well as how they merge.

Chapter 2

Universal Laws? Are They Different Than Getting a Man-made Parking Ticket?

As I have mentioned in chapter 1, nature's laws have always been. They are not something that mankind has made up or fabricated into existence. Universal Laws have formed all of the wonders of nature—from the puzzling perplexity of outer space to the roaring waves of the ocean, including the intelligent, minuet cells that form all of humankind and everything else that's living.

A few of the natural laws that surround us that function without us even being aware of their operation are: the Law of Gravity, the Law of Vibration, or the Law of Rhythms. What goes up must come down. We witness this on a daily basis without even wondering about it. Throw a ball up into the air, and it returns back down to land in a strategic located baseball glove. We don't think about how gravity happens. It's like breathing, it just automatically occurs—actually we count on this law performing its duty to keep us safely grounded on earth. Working with gravity—as in other natural laws—is woven into all movements and happenings of all creatures of the world. Mother Earth will never lose her dressings from floating up and never returning!

Everything is alive and has energy—that is the Law of Vibrations. Everything vibrates at different frequencies. Objects or thoughts with similar vibrations attract to each other. They resonate on the same frequency and thus gravitate toward each other like magnets. As with our thinking, our positive thoughts attract positive things, and negative thoughts draw unto it other negative ideas. The Law of Attraction works with this also. [4AR] Moroni made a comparison of like to like when he said, "For if their works be good, then they are good also." "For behold, God hath said a man being evil cannot do that which is good; . . .." (Moroni 7:5–6).

Like a pendulum that swings from one side to another, the Law of Rhythm establishes the cycles of nature. The bright sun comes up in the morning and sets gently in the late afternoon. Ocean waves come in and blanket the sand and then smoothly go back out to sea. We feel these cycles or rhythms in our daily living. One day we may have a very wonderful day, and the next not so good. From the rhythms of life, we learn to appreciate the good and happy from the sad or frustrated. But being aware of these cycles helps us learn that "this too shall pass" {5} and winter will turn to spring.

The Laws of the Universe, as well as the eternal laws of God, are necessary for life to flourish and mankind to reap happiness and eternal blessings. They don't cost anything in monetary payments or in time figuring out your yearly tax return. They don't change or get modified depending on the need and vote of the people. Universal Laws just are and always have been. You won't find a ticket on your car window from tripping over a rock (gravity law), but you will get a piece of paper on your windshield for parking in the wrong place with man-made laws. Laws that are established to keep the peace or gain money from citizens to pay for road repair. They come and go, depends on the ideas of man. God's laws and natural laws go past the mortal life and reach into forever. Eternal, natural laws, as like the laws of chemistry, state that they can neither be created nor destroyed. {6}

Chapter 3

The Laws are Everywhere Throughout the Scriptures . . . Where's My Highlighter? I'd Like to Mark the Blessings!

Listed in alphabetical order, I have selected only twenty-six out of over one hundred Universal Laws for this informative book. Each law has a definition explaining its function and then a list of chosen scriptures that relate to that natural, eternal law and how it affects our lives when obeyed—our blessings. It may also mention outcomes or benefits. Scriptures researched for this purpose have come from the Bible, Book of Mormon, Doctrine & Covenants (D&C), and Pearl of Great Price.

Hopefully, we will come to a much clearer understanding about which blessings fall under which laws; however, some blessings may apply to more than one law. "For all who will have a blessing at my hands shall abide the law which was appointed for that blessing, and the conditions thereof, as were instituted from before the foundation of the world" (D&C 132:5).

I have chosen a few scriptures per Universal Law listed, realizing that there are many more worded in other ways that may apply under that same law that were not mentioned, but that can be discovered during your own individual study of the scriptures. Bringing up the rear is a short Parable that relates to each law for your imagination to bring to life to farther understanding of the Law.

Honour the Lord with thy substance, and
with the first fruits of all thine increase; So
shall thy barns be filled with plenty, and
thy presses shall burst out with new wine.

—Proverbs 3:9–10

1. The Universal Law of Abundance.

Abundance is all around us and envelops our whole lives. The beauties and varieties of nature cover the globe and bring the abundance of color, texture, sights, and sounds to our everyday living. There is an abundance of air to breath, land to live on and cultivate, water to drink, and God's food to eat. Consider the single apple seed that takes root and grows, matures into a productive apple tree that stems many a hanging juicy apple, which houses multiple seeds inside to sprout many additional trees and fruit. And the processes repeats itself over and over when conditions are right, producing an abundance of fruit for many people. Matthew 13:8 says in parable, "But other fell into good ground, and brought forth fruit, some an hundredfold, some sixtyfold, some thirtyfold."

However, it is up to us to grow the food, find and provide the water, and feed the world—but there is plenty to be found and to spread around when done properly and with sustainability. If you take a moment, you will notice the abundance that you have already in your life—family, friends, time, things you own, knowledge, and much more.

There is always an abundance of wealth. There is not lack, only lack of opportunity and positive thinking. [7AR] When society is caring conscious, there is an abundance of love, charity, and goodwill sustaining cultures and people. Our Heavenly Father and Jesus Christ have an overflowing love for all of us and provides countless blessings when we follow the laws, as well as many tender mercies and miracles to bless our lives. When we obey the laws, we are promised an abundant life producing multitudes of deserved blessings (see listed scriptures below).

Think of the parable of the fishes, when Simon Peter was told to cast his net on the "other side" of the boat, and from his obedience, the fishing party caught a surprising abundance of fish. {8} Or when Jesus was with the multitude and a large amount of food was needed to feed a multitude of people, all from two fishes and five loaves of bread. Yet Jesus blessed the humble offerings in such a way that they ended up in such an overabundance as to feed thousands and still have some food left over. {9} Miracles of abundance are common in the scriptures.

Elder Joseph B. Wirthlin of the Quorum of the Twelve Apostles stated that "the abundant life is a spiritual life." {10} When we strive to follow after Christ and live a righteous life, we recognize more good and abundance around us. Also, "The abundant life involves an endless search for knowledge, light, and truth." {11} Thus, an abundant life develops at our own hands and through our own willing hearts and minds to gain knowledge, care for our physical bodies, show forth love, get out of ourselves, and appreciate the abundance all around us and share it, care for it, and spread more of it to everyone. Second Corinthians 9:6 nicely states, "But this I say, He which soweth sparingly shall reap also sparingly; and he which soweth bountifully shall reap also bountifully."

We have abundance within us. We came to earth already with everything in us to be happy and successful. We were "patent" before we were born as an original individual with multiple talents already housed within ready to be discovered and brought forth for the benefit of ourselves and others. Just look at yourself and recognize the abundance of healthy cells dividing and giving you life, your abundance of emotions that can radiate love and caring, abundance of people all around that you can connect to and share positive happenings, the abundance of smell, sight, touch, and taste that you have to enjoy the beauties of the earth and bring peace to your heart. Realizing this, you must choose abundance in your life, abundance in yourself, and never consider "lack" of anything divine and needful.

Conditions and Blessings in the Scriptures for the Universal Law of Abundance.
(Scriptures have been underlined
and **emphasized**
to help point out the Law and results)

1. **Malachi 3:10** – Payment of Tithing = **Abundance of Blessings**
    Bring ye all the tithes **into the storehouse, that there may be meat in mine house, and prove me now herewith, saith the Lord of host, if I will not open you the windows of heaven, and pour you out a blessing, that there shall not be room enough to receive it.**

2. **D&C 59:10–19** – Keep the Sabbath Day Holy = **Fullness of the Earth**
    For verily this is a day appointed unto you to rest from your labors, and to pay thy devotions unto the Most High; **But remember that on this, the Lord's day, thou shalt** offer thine oblations **and thy sacraments unto the Most High, confessing thy sins unto they brethren, and before the Lord.**
    And on this day thous shalt do none other thing, **only let thy food be prepared with singleness of heart that thy fasting may be per-**

fect, ... And inasmuch as ye do these things with thanksgiving, with cheerful hearts and countenances ... Verily I say, that inasmuch as ye do this, the fullness of the earth is yours, the beasts of the field and the fowls of the air, and that which climbeth upon the trees and walketh upon the earth; Yea, and the herb, and the good things, which come of the earth, whether for food or for raiment, or for houses, or for barns, or for orchards, or for gardens, or for vineyards; Yea, all things which come of the earth, in the season thereof, are made for the benefit and the use of man, both to please the eye and to gladden the heart; Yea, for food and for raiment, for taste and for smell, to strengthen the body and to enliven the soul.

3. Psalms 112:1–3 – <u>Righteousness</u> = **Wealth**

    Praise ye the Lord. <u>Blessed is the man that feareth the Lord</u>**, that delighteth greatly in his commandment. His seed shall be mighty upon earth: the generation of the upright shall be blessed. Wealth and riches shall be in his house: and his righteousness endureth for ever.**

4. Jacob 2:19; Matthew 6:33 – <u>Hope in Christ</u> = **Desired Riches**

    And after ye have <u>obtained a hope in Christ</u> **ye shall obtain riches, if ye seek them; and ye will seek them for the intent to do good—to clothe the naked, and to feed the hungry, and**

to liberate the captive, and administer relief to the sick and the afflicted. But <u>seek ye first the kingdom of God</u>, and his righteousness; and all these things shall be added unto you.

5. Proverbs 3:9–10 – <u>Honour and Giving</u> = **Plenty**
   "<u>Honour the Lord</u> with thy substance, and with the first fruits of all thine increase;" "So shall thy barns be filled with plenty, and thy presses shall burst out with new wine."

6. Isaiah 1:19 – <u>Obedience</u> = **Food**
   "If ye be <u>willing and obedient</u>, ye shall eat the good of the land;"

7. Matthew 6:3–4 – <u>Give Anonymously</u> = **Open Reward**
   "But when thou doest alms, <u>let not thy left hand know what thy right hand doeth;</u>" "That thine alms may be in secret: and thy Father which seeth in secret himself shall reward thee openly."

8. Matthew 13:11–12 – <u>Gospel Knowledge</u> = **Spiritual Abundance**
   He answered and said unto them, Because it is given unto you to <u>know the mysteries of the kingdom of heaven</u>, but to them it is not give. For whosoever hath, to him shall be given, and he shall have more abundance; but whosoever hath not, from him shall be taken away even that he hath.

9. **Deuteronomy 28:47 – S**<u>erve with Joy</u> **= Abundance of all Things (implied)**
    "**Because thou** <u>servedst</u> **not the Lord thy God** <u>with joyfulness,</u> **and with gladness of heart, for the abundance of all things:**"

10. **2 Nephi 4:35 –** <u>Ask</u> **= Liberally Receive**
    "**Yea, I know that God will give liberally to him that** <u>asketh</u>**. Yea, my God will give me, if I ask not amiss; . . .**"

Summary

The Law of Abundance is reflected in the scriptures by the bounty of blessing we will receive when we live according as Christ would have us live—and in a joyous and willing way. Nature grows in unlimited abundance all around us. We have abundance in our lives from day to day if we but just stop and realize how much we have: in love, in family, in the things we have, in our opportunities for growth, and in our possessions. God's love has no end, condition, or limit; it is eternal, and we have that same ability to spread enormous amount of love and caring to all around us. What a wonderful, peaceful world that would be!

There is a maple tree in my backyard that has grown up higher than my upper back deck. When I walk out onto my wooden deck, its thick leafed branches are like out-stretched arms that are ready to embrace me if I just walk forward. Among these green leaves are masses and masses of "helicopter" seeds that the tree has produced ready to let fly when the weather gets cooler in the fall. I am in awe of how many there are! Their abundance is almost overwhelming!

Nature is programmed to reproduce in such high volume to have the greatest possibility of successfully establishing new offspring—be it plants, trees, or flowers. The great multitude of seeds from one single flower is magnificent. Abundance is not lacking in any way, shape, or form.

Abundance in joy, in laughter, and in kindness is embedded deep within our hearts to spread to others. Our "fountain" of positive emotions is constantly replenishing, depending on our thoughts and actions. It continually flows connecting with those around us when we are in the gratitude mentality. The abundance of blessings are around us constantly, be it very small or in spades. When we start counting all the blessings that we have in our lives and the example of multiplicity that nature produces for us, then we become enlightened, we come out of ourselves to really "see" how abundant our world really is. God created so much for us. There is no lack; only lack of appreciation, attitude, and awesomeness.

Parable of Abundance

A certain hiker was walking along a low-shadowed trail surrounded by bushes and established trees with very few flowers growing alongside the firm walkway. Noticing the small few beauties, the hiker assumed that the flowers were getting thinner and scarcer each season. Walking mindlessly ahead, the hiker continued on, not noticing that over the bushes and trees into the open meadow, flowers of the same and more were growing without number, coloring the area beyond amazement.

Photo credit: The Library of Congress via VisualHunt

The desire accomplished is
sweet to the soul . . .

—Proverbs 13:19

2. The Universal Law of Action.

As the title of the law describes, it is a "do, study, and ask" kind of law. It requires some work on our part to accomplish what we are setting out to do. We can't just sit back and "hope" things will come to pass or sit on the couch daydreaming of a life and not do anything about making it manifest itself. Like a movie clapperboard that slams shut as the director announces "Action!" We need to be ready to act our part in making things happen. We are rewarded by our action by getting things done. {12}

Action also is a means by which we improve ourselves and repent or mend our mistakes. Challenges in our lives require maneuvering around roadblocks or climbing over obstacles to move forward and make it through trials—which then enrich our lives. There is always a "silver lining" in every challenging situation that forms our character and integrity.

Everything was and is created by action of thought and action of doing. Nothing just happens. It takes ideas, emotions, and actions to get results. If God just sat on his throne and did nothing, do you think we would be here today, let alone have an eternal home to go to? We were born to work, to survive, to give, and to love.

Think about the magnificent body physic of people who work out, who by their weight-lifting action, perfect the potential of the human body. That takes a devotion and dedication of regular action to accomplish that healthy habit—some actions, or nonactions, are quite noticeable.

Most all the Universal Laws themselves require some sufficient action of some kind to work such as: the Universal Law we just discussed—the Law of Abundance. A person needs to *do* something in order to *get* something. The Law of Action is the law by which guides a person through living or applying any other Universal Law to their life to achieve the prescribed outcome.

The Lord has blessed everyone with talents and abilities that needs to be discovered and developed to be of benefit for that person and for others. As the Parable of the Talents instructs in gaining money or abilities, "And so he that had received five talents came and brought other five talents, saying, Lord, thou deliveredst unto me five talents: behold, I have gained beside them five talents more." "His lord said unto him, Well done, thou good and faithful servant: . . ." As this scriptures teaches, we need to *act* on developing our talents, act on multiplying our worldly means, both for the benefit of reaching our individual potential as well as by way of helping others do the same.

We have been taught through the scriptures that it takes *action* on our part to find and follow the Lord, Jesus Christ. It takes energy and spiritual exertion to recognize the truth, develop faith, be baptized, receive the holy ghost, and endure in righteousness throughout our entire wonderful lives in order to return to our highest position in the eternities. Just standing in one place and looking at the stairs to the golden gate of heaven and not taking the effort to climb up and open it doesn't help at all. But they are beautiful and wondrous to look at if that is all you desire!

Conditions and Blessings in the Scriptures for the Universal Law of Action.

NOTE: The scriptures for the Law of Action will also apply to other Laws of the Universe because all the other eternal laws also require action to manifest such as: the Universal Law of Knowledge or Sowing and Reaping, obviously require action to happen. Plus, there are many scriptures that involve action so just a few are mentioned below.

1. **2 Nephi 9:23** – Baptism and Faith = **Saved**
   "And he commandeth all men that they must repent, and be baptized **in his name, hav-**

ing perfect faith in the Holy One of Israel, or they cannot be saved in the kingdom of God."

2. **D&C 88:118** – <u>Learn and Teach</u> = **More Knowledge**
    "And as all have not faith, <u>seek ye diligently and teach</u> one another words of wisdom; yea, <u>seek ye out</u> of the best books words of wisdom; seek learning, even by study and also by faith."

3. **D&C 88:119** – <u>Prepare</u> = **Spiritual and Organize House**
    <u>Organize</u> yourselves; <u>prepare</u> every needful thing; and <u>establish</u> a house, even a house of prayer, a house of fasting, a house of faith, a house of learning, a house of glory, a house of order, a house of God;

4. **Jacob 2:19** – <u>Riches</u> = **Care for the Needy**
    And <u>after ye have obtained a hope in Christ</u> ye shall obtain riches, <u>if ye seek them;</u> and ye will seek them for the intent to do good – to <u>clothe</u> the naked, and to <u>feed</u> the hungry, and to <u>liberate</u> the captive, and <u>administer</u> relief to the sick and the afflicted.

5. **Genesis 1:1, 27** – <u>Creation</u> = **The Earth, Animals and Man**
    "In the beginning God <u>created</u> the heaven and the earth. So God <u>created</u> man in his own image, in the image of God created he him; male and female created he them."

6. **D&C 58:27** – <u>Good Cause</u> = **Much Righteousness and Blessings**

    Verily I say, men should be <u>anxiously engaged</u> in a good cause, and <u>do</u> many things of their own free will, and <u>bring to pass</u> much righteousness; For the power is in them, wherein they are agents unto themselves. And inasmuch as men do good they shall in nowise lose their reward.

7. **D&C 59:12–13, 16** – <u>Sabbath Oblations</u> = **Fullness and Joy**

    But remember that on this, the Lord's day, thou shalt <u>offer</u> thine oblations and thy sacraments unto the Most High, <u>confessing</u> thy sins unto thy brethren, and before the Lord. And on this day thou shalt do none other thing, only let thy food be <u>prepared</u> with singleness of heart that thy <u>fasting</u> may be perfect, or, in other words, that thy joy may be full. Verily I say, that inasmuch as ye do this, the fulness of the earth is yours . . .

8. **Revelations 2:19** – <u>Good Works</u> = **Acknowledgment**

    "I know thy <u>works,</u> and <u>charity,</u> and <u>service,</u> and <u>faith,</u> and thy <u>patience,</u> and thy <u>works;</u> . . ."

9. **D&C 9:8–9** <u>Study and Ask</u> = **Answer**

    But, behold, I say unto you, that you must <u>study</u> it out in your mind; then you must <u>ask</u> me if it be right, and if it is right I will cause that your bosom shall burn within you; therefore,

you shall feel that it is right. But if it be not right you shall have no such feelings, but you shall have a stupor of thought that shall cause you to forget the thing which is wrong; . . .

10. **Moroni 10:3–4** – <u>Ponder and Ask</u> = **Receive Truth**

    Behold, I would exhort you that when ye shall <u>read</u> these things…..and <u>ponder</u> it in your heart.

    And when ye shall receive these things, (words of God) I would exhort you that ye would <u>ask</u> God, the Eternal Father, in the name of Christ, if these things are not true; and if ye shall <u>ask with a sincere heart, with real intent, having faith</u> **in Christ, he will manifest the truth of it unto you, by the power of the Holy Ghost.**

Summary

The Law of Action is a "must" to be able to accomplish anything at all, worthwhile or not. It requires movement, energy, thought, learning, asking, giving, creating. To reach our potential in mortality and earn or receive an eternal reward, it requires faith, repentance, forgiveness, and gratitude. Life is an existence of energy and movement, of vibrations and functioning to love and be loved. Every natural and eternal law relies on the Law of Action to accomplish the purpose of its being. Nothing stands still. Everything is in movement as the Law of Vibration describes. [13 AR] Every other natural or eternal law breaths action to life.

Can anything living be of any use not producing or not contributing to life? Can we humans be of any use if we just decide to idle away our time and become a "couch potato," imprinting our backsides into a four-legged human support unit? To do anything, we must make the effort to move. If we have a goal or dream to accomplish anything worthwhile, we must accelerate ourselves into action and make or create what we want. Actually, it can go the opposite direction as well. To do anything meaningless or mischievous, it takes a fair amount of action as well.

Service to our fellow man takes action. Righteousness in our hearts and minds calls our spirits into action to produce good things, grand ideas, and steps in the right direction for human happiness. Even taking the initiative to improve ourselves and recognizing that we can requires a constant, dedicated effort on our part—a glorious movement, an attractive action that draws only good things to us. Move forward. Take action and become our best selves, our honest selves, and intelligent selves—it is much, much better than doing nothing!

Parable of Action

An average person with visions of dreams a possibility, found their chair quite comfortable and safe, with goals spinning around in the air never landing—always anticipating. Whereas another aspiring person took hold of their imagined dreams, pulled them into their heart, rose from their chair, and worked. Every dream they envisioned came true.

Photo credit: Eric Kilby via Visual hunt / CC BY-SA

> Associate yourself with men of good quality
> if you esteem yourself own reputation. It
> is better be alone than in bad company.
>
> —George Washington

3. The Universal Law of Association.

This law has to do with our association with people. Basically, you become like those with whom you spend time with. Granted everyone has a different personality, but one seems to pick up ways of thinking, dressing styles, attitudes, ideas, and morals from the people they spend the most time with. [14AR]

Either for good or ill, our friends can influence us for better or for worse. They either support us in our quest for self-improvement, or they innocently sabotage our efforts.

Take trying to eat healthier. When going out for lunch, do we stick to our plan of eating more vegetables, or do we cave in to the promptings of our friends to eat something unhealthy and loaded with calories? "You are, after all, eating out with your best buds, and you can always eat another way tomorrow." It is much easier and more effective if you just choose a lunch companion that wants to be healthy also and supports the idea of consuming fresh greens.

Never underestimate the power another person can have on yourself, especially if you are around them quite often. You need to be around people that inspire you, that lift you up, and that vibrates on a positive level. This positive or negative sway can be very subtle without you even noticing it. If a person was alarming in their behavior and offensive, then you would probably back away quickly, but hints of degradation can be very small and hardly noticeable. And that is how Satan works to catch you in his snare {15} a little at a time, in small questionable actions and offensive language.

Take for instance, the "slick tongued" lawyers or leaders in some of the Book of Mormon stories that used flattering words to convince the people to go their way. Korihor, in the book of Alma, used flattering words to effectively move the people away from righteousness. When debating with the great righteous disciple of God, Alma referred to Korihor's deceitful language, "Should be lost than that thou shouldst be the means of bringing many souls down to destruction, by thy lying and by they flattering words," (Alma 30:47).

On the other hand, wonderful words of God can lead many individuals toward righteousness and goodness. "And now, as the preaching of the word had a great tendency to lead the people to do that which was just—yea, it had had more powerful effect upon the minds of the people than the sword, or anything else," (Alma 31:5).

As the saying goes, "Birds of a feather, flock together," exactly summarizes the effect of people on our lives and who we are attracted to. Peer pressure is a heavy influence, and thus it is vital that we choose friends and associates that radiate goodness and integrity. In fact, we need to make sure our own personality and ideas of morality attracts people with high values and ideas of the same. Even in the arena of achieving goals, one needs to focus on mingling with likeminded individuals that are working at bettering themselves and reaching their potential as well and letting go of people that are thinking the opposite. [16AR]

Influences of Different People in the Scriptures— Be It for Good or for Ill—for the Universal Law of Association

1. **4 Nephi 1:2–5 –** All with Christ **= Peace, Equality, Miracles**

   The people were all converted unto the Lord, **upon all the face of the land, both Nephites and Lamanites, and there were no contentions and disputations among them, and every man did deal justly one with another. And they had all things common among them; therefore there were not rich and poor, bond and free, but they were all made free, and partakers of the heavenly gift. And there were great and marvelous works** wrought by the disciples of Jesus, Insomuch that they did heal the sick, and raise the dead, and cause the lame to walk, and the blind to receive their sight, and the deaf to hear; and all manner of miracles did they work among the children of men; and in nothing did they work miracles save it were in the name of Jesus.

2.   4 Nephi 1:15–18 –With love of God = Peace, Blessings, Prosperity

And it came to pass that there was no contention in the land, because of the love of God which did dwell in the hearts of the people. And there were no envyings, nor strifes, nor tumults, nor whoredoms, nor lyings, nor murders, nor any manner of lasciviousness; and surely there could not be a happier people among all the people who had been created by the hand of God. There were no robbers, nor murderers, neither were there Lamanites, nor any manner of -ites; but they were in one, the children of Christ, and heirs to the kingdom of God. And how blessed were they! For the Lord did bless them in all their doings; yea, even they were blessed and prospered . . .

3.   4 Nephi 1:34, 38, 39 – Led by False Priests = Iniquity, Wrong Teachings, Broken into Tribes.

Nevertheless, the people did harden their hearts, for they were led by many priests and false prophets to build up many churches, . . .

And it came to pass that they who <u>rejected the gospel</u> were called Lamanites, and Lemuelites, and Ishmaelites; and they did not dwindle in unbelief, but they did willfully rebel against the gospel of Christ; and they did teach their children that they should not believe, even as their fathers, from the beginning, did dwindle. And they were taught to hate the children of God, even as the Lamanites were taught to hate the children of Nephi from the beginning.

4. Ruth 1:16 – <u>Loyalty</u> = **Togetherness and Kinship**
    And Ruth said, Intreat me <u>not to leave thee</u>, or to return from following after thee: for <u>whither thou goest,</u> I will go; and <u>where thou lodgest</u>, I will lodge: thy people shall be my people, and thy God my God:

5. Isaiah 13:14 – <u>Own People</u> = **Own Land**
    "They shall every man<u> turn </u>to his own people, and <u>flee every one</u> into his own land."

6. Jeremiah 5:23 – <u>Revolting and Rebellious</u> = **Gone**
    "But this people hath a <u>revolting and a rebellious heart;</u> they are revolted and gone."

7. Revelation 21:2–3 – <u>People of God</u> = **God as Their Leader**
    And I John saw the <u>holy city, new Jerusalem, coming down from God</u> out of heaven, <u>prepared</u> as a bride adorned for her husband. And I heard a great voice out of heaven saying, Behold, the

tabernacle of God is with men, and he will dwell with them, and they shall be his people, and God himself shall be with them, and be their God.

8. 2 Nephi 5:5–6, 8–9, 13–14 – God's people, the Nephites = **Prosperity,**
    And it came to pass that the Lord did warn me, that I, Nephi, should depart from them and flee into the wilderness, and all those who would go with me. Wherefore, it came to pass that I, Nephi, did take my family, and also Zoram and his family, and Sam, mine elder brother and his family, and Jacob and Joseph, my younger brethren, and also my sisters, and all those who would go with me. And all those who would go with me were those who believed in the warnings and the revelations of God; wherefore, they did hearken unto my words. And my people would that we should call the name of the place Nephi; wherefore, we did call it Nephi. And all those who were with me did take upon them to call themselves the people of Nephi. And it came to pass that we began to prosper exceedingly, and to multiply in the land.

9. Heleman 11:24–26 – Enemies to God = **Destruction and Murder**
    There were a certain number of the dissenters from the people of Nephi, who had some years before gone over unto the Lamanites, and taken

upon themselves the name of Lamanites, and also a certain number who were real descendants of the Lamanites, <u>being stirred up to anger by them</u>, or by those dissenters, therefore <u>they commenced a war</u> with their brethren. And they did commit murder and plunder; and then they would retreat back into the mountains, and into the wilderness and secret places, hiding themselves that they could not be discovered, receiving daily an addition to their numbers, inasmuch as there were dissenters that went forth unto them. And thus in time, yea, even in the space of not many years, they became an exceedingly great band of robbers; and they did search out all the secret plans of Gadianton; and thus they became robbers of Gadianton.

10. 3 Nephi 7:2–5 – <u>Divisions of Tribes</u> = Contention and Wickedness

And the people were <u>divided one against another</u>; and they did <u>separate one from another into tribes, every man according to his family and his kindred, and friends</u>; and thus they did destroy the government of the land. and every tribe did appoint a chief or leader over them; and thus they became tribes and leaders of tribes. Now behold, there was no man among them save he had much family and many kindreds and friends; therefore their tribes became exceedingly great. Now all this was done, and there were no wars as yet among them; and all

this iniquity had come upon the people because they <u>did yield themselves unto the power of Satan.</u>

Summary

We must always be aware of the people we are around in our everyday happenings. Some people carry wonderful vibrations of joy and love, while others slump around dragging complaints and bad ideas. Our associations can play a big part on our personal development toward either higher levels of goodness or lower levels of negativeness. That is why choosing our friends wisely is important. You might add or suggest that if my example is good enough, then I may be able to change the other person whom I am associating with. And perhaps my presence "often enough" will persuade positive results from them on to myself. Being a good example and displaying positive vibrations is vital to attract other positive people, but perhaps you need to do it from afar; otherwise, even with good intentions, you may be playing Russian Roulette and end up having it backfire on you and you being the one that was changed to degrading behavior. This is a dangerous way of thinking and usually has a boomerang effect; however, in the case with loved ones, we do hope our positive influence will rub off and touch their hearts. Something that we definitely need to keep applying—our love and acceptance. Living a righteous life is always desirable, and people do have a change of heart, just check the people whom you spend the most time with, associates who are also righteous and uplifting to you and you to them.

There are so many different people in the world with all kinds of beliefs and traditions. We can learn a lot from each other. And I believe down deep that we all can feel and know what is good and what is not desirable among ourselves. Traveling can teach us much about each other and our interesting life stories. But for those we associate often and continually, needs to be persons that lift us, teach us goodness, and bring our souls to high levels of peace, love, and joy.

Parable of Association

A young bird with a developing voice saw two flocks of older birds with definite sounds. The one group sang sweet tunes that entertained the trees, and the other group produced squawks that the weeds enjoyed. The future tunes from the young bird were decided at the moment of what part of nature to entertain.

Photo credit: Philippe Put via Visual Hunt / CC BY

Mind is the Master power that moulds
and makes, And Man is Mind, and
evermore he takes The tool of Thought,
and, shaping what he wills, Brings forth
a thousand joys, a thousand ills:—He
thinks in secret, and it comes to pass:
Environment is but his looking-glass.

—James Allen, 1864–1912

4. The Universal Law of Attraction/Vibration.

This law is kind of obvious. You get what you ask for or
what you think about or what your ideas and attitudes
are. Just like a magnet that attracts metal things to it, you
attract to yourself positive things or negative things. If

you naturally have love in your countenance, then that is what you will demonstrate to those around you, thus love and kindness will flow back to you. Your vibrations either high or low will attract like vibrations of the same. Peace, love, and joy dwell at the upper levels and conflict, complaining, and ingratitude gravitate toward the polar end of goodness. [17AR]

What your mind concentrates on is what will manifest in your life. If I loved to read, for example, then I would have lots of reading materials around me in the venue I enjoyed most and even perhaps become an author myself on the same subject—lo and behold. Be so doing, I attract sources of more reading materials and will take notice of new authors who talk on the same subject I am interested in, thus I learn even more.

You will notice this quite often if you think about it. Golfers will attract other golfing buddies. Artists group together, set up easels on green hillsides and paint together. Surfers ride the waves alongside each other, and wealthy individuals attract wealth if they think and plan and take action. This Law of Attraction is similar to the Law of Association. Whom we associate with also attracts the same kind of individuals or vice versa.

This law also has a negative effect, depending on what we concentrate on. If we focus our minds on "lack"—of this or that—then "lack" is what we will get. That is why it is important to take notice of how we "talk" to ourselves. If I keep telling myself that I am not good enough and I can't do something, then I never will. If I am shy and afraid to talk to someone or step forward, then it's likely that I never will, because that is what I am thinking about—fear, low self-esteem, or not enough love for myself, consequently that is what I attract to myself if I desire it or not.

So how do I get out of that scenario? *Think positive!* Think about what you *want* and not what you *don't* want. If I want more happiness, then think and do more things that brings my heart more joy and to others, a brighter smile. Then more positive, happy things will come my way. What you spread around is what will be attracted back to you. This is also what the Universal Law of Sowing and Reaping is all about (see the Law of Cause and Effect). It is interesting how some Universal Laws are entwined into each other or go side by side.

The scriptures tell us situations where this law is manifest. Good righteous people of God attract righteousness and Godliness. People of God who believe the same are attracted to each other and support each other in righteousness and in honoring God. Where the reverse is also true. Those who have a hard heart or evil intentions attract evil happenings into their lives and attract others with the same ideas and cunning ways.

You get what you think about most, be it good or bad, positive or negative, progressing or digressing. Thoughts can change once you become aware of them and realize that they are just preprogrammed ideas or habits that are not what you desire to become better. It does take effort, but it is possible. Our minds can change and mold into another state if we want them to. Just change your thinking to what you *want* and concentrate in a very committed way daily, and sooner or later, your mind will transform into a new way of thinking, and desired results will be attracted to you. Always focus on solutions, not problems. Focus on "I Can," not "I Can't," and focus on your blessings and abundance and never, ever, on what you don't have or the "lack" of things. Remember, you attract what you think about and what your character is—be it kindness of word and action or doubt and murmuring.

Influences of Good or Ill by Whom or What We Attract—for the
Universal Law of Attraction/Vibration

1. **Mosiah 5:2 –** Belief **= Change of Heart/ Surety**
    And they all cried with one voice, **saying: Yea, we** believe **all the words which thous hast spoken unto us; and also, we know of their surety and truth, because of the Spirit of the Lord Omnipotent, which has wrought a mighty change in us, or in our hearts, that we have no more disposition to do evil, but to do good continually.**

2. **Alma 5:40; 3 Nephi 14:17 –** Good **= Good,** Evil **= Evil**
    For I say unto you that whatsoever is good **cometh from God, and whatsoever is** evil **cometh from the devil. Even so every** good tree **bringeth forth good fruit; but a** corrupt tree **bringeth forth evil fruit.**

3. **Alma 32:35 –** Light **= Good**
    O then, is not this real? I say unto you, Yea, because it is light; and whatsoever is light, **is good, because it is discernible, therefore ye must know**

that it is good; and now behold, after ye have tasted this light is your knowledge perfect?

4. **Alma 40:13 –** Evil = **Darkness**
    And then shall it come to pass, that the spirits of the wicked, yea, who are evil—**for behold, they have** no part nor portion of the Spirit of the Lord; **for behold, they chose evil works rather than good; therefore the spirit of the devil did enter into them, and take possession of their house—and these shall be cast out into outer darkness; there shall be weeping, and wailing, and gnashing of teeth, and this** because of their own iniquity, **being led captive by the will of the devil.**

5. **Ether 4:11–12 –** Truth = **Good**
    But he that believeth these things **which I have spoken, him will I visit with the manifestations of my Spirit, and he shall know and bear record. For** because of my Spirit **he shall know that these things are true;** for it persuadeth man **to do good. And whatsoever** thing persuadeth men to do good **is of me; for good cometh of none save it be of me . . .**

6. **Moroni 7:13 –** God = **Good**
    "But behold, that which is of God **inviteth and enticeth to do good continually; wherefore,** every thing which inviteth and enticeth to do good, **and to** love God, and to serve him, **is inspired of God."**

7. **Jacob 5:37** – <u>Wild Branches</u> = **Evil Fruit**

But behold, the <u>wild branches have grown and have overrun</u> the roots thereof; and because that the wild branches have overcome the roots thereof it hath brought forth much evil fruit; and because that it hath brought forth so much evil fruit thou beholdest that it beginneth to perish; and it will soon become ripened, that it may be cast into the fire, except we should do something for it to preserve it.

8. **D&C 10:21** – <u>Corruption</u> = **Darkness**

"And their <u>hearts are corrupt,</u> and full of wickedness and abominations; and they <u>love darkness</u> rather than light, because <u>their deeds</u> are evil; therefore they will not ask of me."

9. **Moroni 7:17** – <u>Deny God</u> = **Service the Devil**

But whatsoever thing <u>persuadeth men</u> to do evil, and believe not in Christ, and deny him, and serve not God, then ye may know with a perfect knowledge it is of the devil; for after this manner doth the devil work, <u>for he persuadeth</u> no man to do good, no, not one; neither do his angels; neither do they who subject themselves unto him.

10. **D&C 90:24** – <u>Prayer and Belief</u> = **All Things for your Good**

"<u>Search diligently, pray always, and be believing,</u> and all things shall work together for your

good, if ye <u>walk uprightly</u> **and remember the covenant wherewith ye have** <u>covenanted one with another.</u>"

Summary

The Law of Attraction is exactly what it emphasizes—you get what you think about, be it positive and good or negative and nonproductive. It's as simple as that. There are many choices of thoughts to be on display within our minds at any given time, so just becoming aware of what they are is a vital choice of action to a positive outcome in our lives.

The upside-down pyramid of vibrations only widen at the top the more we focus our attention onto positive, generous, and loving things. {18} War and sludge vibrations aren't very wide and settle on the bottom, not leaving room for anything godly.

Being righteous and believing in our eternal nature and in our Heavenly Father attracts an abundance of goodness in our hearts that will flow into our lives more of the same; thus, we receive a multitude of blessings through obedience and a pure heart. Living our lives on a high level of happiness and prosperity is a much desired way of existence.

Recognizing that the opposite feeling of heart is as much a possibility is very important to continuously choosing a higher way of life—and to achieving a higher place in our life hereafter. Being attracted to nonconstructive thinking or because of pollutant ideas that we may generate, we attract much of the same. We get what we think about. Negative thinking is a very dangerous game to play.

Parable of Attraction/Vibration

It seems that when blood is put into the ocean where sharks dwell, that they come from far regions to that location. It seems that when intentions are put into the water of action that the same kind of intentions from others appear in response.

Photo credit: TumblingRun via Visualhunt.com / CC BY-ND

> Therefore I say unto you, what things
> soever ye desire, when ye pray, believe that
> ye receive them, and ye shall have them.

—Mark 11:24

5. The Universal Law of Belief.

Henry Ford advised, "Whether you think you can or you think you can't you are right." The Law of Belief is such that what you put into your mind, especially your subconscious mind, will manifest itself in the real world. What I believe I can do will be the results that I receive through my actions and behavior. If I believe that I can ride a bicycle, and I practice long enough, even though I may fall over multiple times in the process, I *will* succeed—because I believe I could.

From an unknown author, "You don't believe what you see, you rather see what you have already decided to believe." The Law of Belief is vital to do pretty much anything. If you don't think or believe you can do anything, then you wouldn't—you would just sit and vegetate and accomplish nothing. Life would be worthless. But since we have the power to believe we can do anything, then with action, we can. [19AR]

Belief is just a thought that I am sure about, positive about and converted about—be it good or bad. The quality of performance is determined by how well one believes in the action. Athletes believe in themselves. They believe they can perform well because they have paid the price of continuous practice to do the best that they are able to do. Like the little train that needed to climb a very steep hill, it just repeated to itself, "I think I can! I think I can! I think I can!" and then after reaching the top tooted, "I thought I could! I thought I could!" {20}

Most all the things that we do in life that we succeed at are achieved by how well we believe that we can accomplish what we want or want to do. Even through the accomplishment of baking a loaf of fresh bread. A cook believes that they are very skilled and capable of doing such a thing and then, without even thinking much about it, soon the result is a load of baked, golden brown bread—its aroma permeating from room to room. All through the belief and confidence from the baker about his capabilities and cooking know-how. From this we also need to add that an individual that does not yet have necessary skills can still have the belief that they are capable of acquiring them.

The Law of Belief also entails actual belief in something that is not seen but hoped for, such as belief in a heavenly being, an eternal Father. Or a belief that God's laws are for our happiness, benefit and eternal salvation. It is an action of faith. Alma in the Book of Mormon taught, "And now as I said concerning faith—faith is not to have a perfect knowledge of things; therefore if ye have faith ye hope for things which are not seen, which are true" (Alma 32:21). To know for a surety, or a definite fact, then we are past belief and faith, and we have attained exact knowledge—a sure knowledge. "Yea, they shall know of a surety that these things are true, for from heaven will I declare it unto them" (D&C 5:12).

We pray to a wonderful, loving God that we have not seen, yet we believe in His existence. We may also get confirmation on our beliefs from other witnesses in the scriptures that have seen Him. The scriptures teach us valuable lessons about the Gospel through the lives of past generations. We did not see or live among them, but we believe that they existed, and their stories benefit us by their examples and their beliefs.

Blessings or Consequences in the Scriptures for the Universal Law of Belief

1. **Mark 11:23–24** – <u>Desire & Believe</u> = **Receive**

   For verily I say unto you, That whosoever <u>shall say</u> unto this mountain, Be thou removed, and be thou cast into the sea; and <u>shall not doubt in his heart,</u> but <u>shall believe</u> that those things which he saith shall come to pass; he shall have whatsoever he saith.

   Therefore I say unto you, <u>What things soever ye desire, when ye pray, believe that ye receive them,</u> and ye shall have them.

2. **Moroni 7:26** – <u>Ask</u> = **Receive**

   "**Whatsoever thing** <u>ye shall ask</u> **the Father in my name,** <u>which is good, in faith believing that ye shall receive,</u> **behold, it shall be done unto you.**"

3. **2 Nephi 33:10** – <u>Believe in Christ</u> = **Believe His Words**

   And now, my beloved brethren, and also Jew, and all ye ends of the earth, <u>hearken unto these words and believe in Christ</u>; and if ye believe not in these words believe in Christ, And if ye shall believe in Christ ye will believe in these words, for they are the words of Christ, and he hath given them unto me; and they teach all men that they should do good.

4. **Mosiah 4:9–10** – <u>Believe in God</u> = **Believe He Can Forgiveness**

    <u>Believe in God; believe that he is</u>, **and** <u>that he created all things</u>, **both in heaven and in earth;** <u>believe that he has all wisdom</u>, **and all power, both in heaven and in earth; believe that man doth not comprehend all the things which the Lord can comprehend.**

    And again, <u>believe</u> **that ye must repent of your sins and forsake them, and humble yourselves before God; and ask in sincerity of heart that he would forgive you; and now, if you believe all these things see that ye do them.**

5. **Moroni 7:16–17** – <u>Belief in God</u> = **Goodness,** <u>Not Belief in God</u> = **Evil**

    For behold, the Spirit of Christ is given to every man, that <u>he may know good from evil</u> **wherefore, I show unto you the way to judge; for** <u>everything which inviteth to do good,</u> **and to** <u>persuade to believe in Christ,</u> **is sent forth by the power and gift of Christ; wherefore ye may know with a perfect knowledge it is of God. But** <u>whatsoever thing persuadeth men to do evil, and believe not in Christ</u>, **and deny him, and serve not God, then ye may know with a perfect knowledge it is of the devil; for after this manner doth the** <u>devil work, for he persuadeth</u> **no man to do good, no, not one; neither do his angel; neither do they who subject themselves unto him.**

6. **D&C 35:8–9** – <u>Believe</u> = **Receive Miracles**
    And I will show miracles, signs, and won-ders, <u>unto all those who believe</u> on my name.

    And whoso <u>shall ask it in my name in faith,</u> **they shall cast out devils; they shall heal the sick; they shall cause the blind to receive their sight, and the deaf to hear, and the dumb to speak, and the lame to walk.**

7. **D&C 90:24** – <u>Believe</u> = **Things Will Work For Your Goodness**
    "<u>Search diligently, pray always, and be believ-ing,</u> and all things shall work together for your good, if ye walk uprightly and remember the covenant wherewith ye have covenanted one with another."

8. **Alma 32:16, 18** – <u>Those Who Believe</u> = **Are Blessed**
    Therefore, blessed are they <u>who humble themselves</u> **without being compelled to be hum-ble; or rather, in other words, blessed is he** <u>that believeth in the word of God</u>**, and is baptized without stubbornness of heart, yea, without being brought to know the word, or even com-pelled to know, before they will believe. Now I ask, is this faith? Behold, I say unto you, Nay; for if a man knoweth a thing he hath no cause to believe, for he knoweth it.**

9. **Alma 32:27** – <u>Try to Believe</u> = **Desire to Believe**
    But behold, if ye will <u>awake and arouse your faculties, even to an experiment upon my words,</u>

and exercise a particle of faith, **yea, even if ye can no more than** desire to believe, **let this desire work in you, even until ye believe in a manner that ye can give place for a portion of my words.**

10. **D&C 8:10** – Faith and Belief = **Action**
   "**Remember that without faith** you can do nothing; **therefore ask in faith. Trifle not with these things; do not ask for that which you ought not.**"

Summary

The Universal Law of Belief states that whatever a person holds in their mind, be it true or not, will manifest itself into reality through their actions and behavior. To believe in oneself is to have confidence in our abilities to accomplish anything, and when we do, the results in our lives will hold true according to what we believe is possible. If a person believes in truth, love, and joy, then that is how they will live as part of their character—which will be noticeable with how they communicate with others around them. But if a person has a misconstrued belief that it's okay to lie, cheat, and be dishonest, then that will be manifest in their behavior toward anyone else that comes into their mortal realm. It is quite simple or easy to get an idea of how another person believes just by seeing them live or function in their lives from day to day. Everything we do originates from a learned or taught belief, either in ourselves and our ability to perform or in someone else, such as a higher being.

   In order to reach the level of performance perfection in playing an instrument, for example, one must have the faith and belief in themselves to stick it out long enough to achieve such ability. All living creatures run on the belief that they can hunt for food, care for young ones, or run from danger. Instinct, yes, but also belief that it's even possible. I believe that we are programmed, so to speak, to believe in ourselves to a certain extent in order to get along in life and accomplish anything. But then we also need to rid ourselves of beliefs that are false or holding us back. Perhaps ideas that we received in childhood about ourselves that could have been more positive when now, as an adult, we need to reevaluate and extinguish, developing new and more producing ones. [21AR]

The Lord's Gospel laws requires one to have faith and belief in order to accomplish needed actions or covenants to return to him, even when we have not seen with our eyes, but only with our hearts. Our earthly existence was meant to teach us faith to cause us to believe and trust in his name. When we hold truth and love in our hearts by following Christ, then that is what will come back to us, and we will receive blessings for doing so.

Parable of Belief

There was a certain man with a bicycle that needed to reach a challenging location. Without knowing exactly what lay ahead and what would be required to end his destination, he peddled ahead. Mile after mile, through fog, rain, and mud, he persevered without turning back until he succeeded, not because he had the ability, but because he believed he did.

Photo credit: toddwendy via VisualHunt / CC BY

> Every thought is a course and every
> condition is an effect. Change your
> thoughts and you change your destiny.
>
> —Joseph Murphy

6. The Universal Law of Cause and Effect.

Most of the other Universal Laws play around this law. Such as the Law of Sow and Reap, or the Law of Attraction, this Universal Law of Cause and Effect is merged into both of them—basically, it is that what you wish for or think about is what you will get. So you need to be careful for what you wish for. Every action has an opposite reaction. The wind blows, and the trees move. [22AR]

For an example, if you put in a lot of hard work to build muscle—which is the cause—then the effect will be a firmer body. If you take the time to plow, pull out weeds, plant the vegetable seeds, water and care for your healthy garden, then at harvest time, you will reap the rewards of a bounteous harvest of nutritional food. The effect of "I earned a lot of money" was caused by the effort you put into accumulating it. When you create a cause, then it universally will bring a result, the effect.

As with everything else, the opposite is also valid. If you create chaos or disorder, then you will reap or achieve the effect of being unsettled or disruptive or worse, depending on how negative the cause was meant to be. Many stories in the scriptures relate to people who are either communicating righteousness causes which bring about the effect of peaceful living or hatefulness causes which produces war and destruction.

It is interesting that in our own world or sphere of existence that we live in from day to day is a product of our own cause and effect. From our own beliefs, from our own actions, from our own thoughts and outcomes. "I caused the thought to purchase a home and I took action to make it legal and binding and so now I dwell in a place I chose to reside in." From my thoughts, to my actions, to my causes, resulting in my results. Whatever we put out there and set in motion will manifest itself sooner or later, depending on how much effort we put into it to materialize. We are the master of our hearts and the master of our souls and the master of our lives.

Blessings or Consequences in the Scriptures for the Universal Law of Cause and Effect

1. Genesis 3:3–6, 11–12, 22–23 - <u>Eat the Forbidden Fruit</u> = **Fall from Eden, Mankind Began**

    But of the fruit of the tree which is in the midst of the garden, God hath said, Ye shall <u>not eat of it, neither shall ye touch it,</u> lest ye die. And the serpent said unto the woman, Ye shall not surely die:

    For God doth know that in the day ye eat thereof, then your eyes shall be opened, and ye shall be as god, knowing good and evil. And when the woman saw that the tree was good for food, and that it was pleasant to the eyes, and a tree to be desired to make one wise, she <u>took of the fruit thereof, and did eat, and gave also unto her husband with her; and he did eat.</u> And he said, Who told thee that thou wast naked? Hast thou eaten of the tree, whereof I commanded thee that thou shouldest not eat?:

    And the man said, The woman whom thou gavest to be with me, she gave me of the tree, and I did eat. And the Lord God said, Behold, the man is become as one of us, to know good and evil: and now, lest he put forth his hand, and take also of the tree of life, and eat, and live forever: Therefore the Lord God sent him forth from the garden of Eden, to till the ground from whence he was taken.

2. **Alma 41:3–6 –** <u>Good</u> **= Good,** <u>Evil</u> **= Evil**

    And it is requisite with the justice of God that men should be judged according to their works; and <u>if their works were good</u> **in this life, and the** <u>desires of their hearts were good,</u> **that they should also, at the last day, be restored unto that which is good.** <u>And if their works are evil</u> **they shall be restored unto them for evil. Therefore, all things shall be restored to their proper order, every thing to its natural frame – mortality raised to immortality, corruption to incorruption—raised to endless happiness to inherit the kingdom of God, or to endless misery to inherit the kingdom of the devil, the one on one hand, the other on the other. The one raised to happiness** <u>according to his desires of happiness,</u> **or good according to his desires of good; and the other to evil** <u>according to his desires of evil;</u> **for as he has** <u>desired to do evil</u> **all the day long even so shall he have his reward of evil when the night cometh. And so it is on the other hand. If he hath repented of his sins, and** <u>desired righteousness</u> **until the end of his days, even so he shall be rewarded unto righteousness.**

3. **Alma 12:31 –** <u>Action</u> **= Good or Evil**

    Wherefore, he gave commandments unto men, they having first transgressed the first commandments as to things which were temporal, and becoming as God, knowing good from evil, <u>placing themselves in a state to act,</u> **or**

being placed in a state to act according to their wills and pleasures, whether to do evil or to do good.

4. **Mosiah 5:2** – <u>Change of Heart</u> = **Desire to do Goodness**

    And they all cried with one voice, saying: Yea, <u>we believe all the words</u> **which thou hast spoken unto us; and also,** <u>we know of their surety and truth</u>**, because of the Spirit of the Lord Omnipotent, which has wrought a mighty change in us, or in our hearts, that we have no more disposition to do evil, but to do good continually.**

5. **Moroni 7:6–10, 12–13** – <u>Evil Gift</u> = **Evil**

    For behold, God hath said a man being evil cannot do that which is good for it he offereth a gift, or prayeth unto God, <u>except he shall do it with real intent</u> **it profiteth him nothing. For behold, it is not counted unto him for righteousness. For behold,** <u>if a man being evil giveth a gift, he doeth it grudgingly;</u> **wherefore it is counted unto him the same as if he had retained the gift; wherefore he is counted evil before God. And likewise also is it counted evil unto a man, if he** <u>shall pray and not with real intent</u> **of heart; yea, and it profiteth him nothing, for God receiveth none such. Wherefore, a man being evil cannot do that which is good; neither will he give a good gift.**

6. **Moroni 7:12–13 –** <u>Goodness</u> **= Inspired of God**
    Wherefore, all things which are good <u>com-</u><u>eth of God;</u> **and that which is evil** <u>cometh of the</u> <u>devil;</u> **for** <u>the devil</u> **is an enemy unto God, and fighteth against him continually, and inviteth and enticeth to sin, and to do that which is evil continually. But behold,** <u>that which is of God</u> **inviteth and enticeth to do good continually; wherefore, every thing which inviteth and enticeth to do good, and to love God, and to serve him,** <u>is inspired of God.</u>

7. **D&C 58:28 –** <u>Do Good</u> **= Reward**
    "For the <u>power is in them, wherein they are</u> <u>agents unto themselves.</u> **And inasmuch as** <u>men</u> <u>do good</u> **they shall in nowise lose their reward."**

8. **Mormon 1:16–19 –** <u>Evil</u> **= No Teachings From Disciples**
    And I did endeavor to preach unto this people, but my mouth was shut, and I was forbidden that I should preach unto them; for behold they had <u>willfully rebelled against their God;</u> **and the beloved** <u>disciples were taken away</u> **out of the land, because of their iniquity. But I did remain among them, but I was forbidden to preach unto them, because of the hardness of their hearts; and because of the** <u>hardness of their</u> <u>hearts the land was cursed</u> **for their sake. And these Gadianton robbers, who were among the Lamanites, did infest he land, insomuch that**

the inhabitants thereof began to hide up their treasures in the earth; and they became slippery, because the Lord had cursed the land, that they could not hold them, nor retain them again. And it came to pass that there were sorceries, and witchcrafts, and magics; and the power of the evil one was wrought upon all the face of the land, even unto the fulfilling of all the words of Abinadi, and also Samuel the Lamanite.

9. **3 Nephi 27:19–20** – Baptism = **Kingdom of God**

   And no unclean thing can **enter into his kingdom; therefore nothing entereth into his rest save it be those who have washed their garments in my blood, because of their** faith, and the repentance of all their sins, and their faithfulness unto the end. **Now this is the commandment:** Repent, **all ye ends of the earth, and** come unto me and be baptized in my name, **that ye may be sanctified by the reception of the Holy Ghost, that ye may stand spotless before me at the last day.**

10. **D&C 89:18–20** – Obey Word of Wisdom = **Better Health, Wisdom**

    And all saints who remember to keep and do these sayings, walking in obedience to the commandments, **shall receive health in their navel and morrow to their bones; And shall find wisdom and great treasures of knowledge,**

even hidden treasures; And shall run and not be weary, and shall walk and not faint. And I, the Lord, give unto them a promise, that the destroying angel shall pass by them, as the children of Israel, and not slay them. Amen.

Summary

The Universal Law of Cause and Effect runs through our lives pretty much constantly. The actions that we do throughout the hours in a day creates an effect or a result. When we prepare a meal, we set up a condition where we need to wash the dishes afterward. The food also gives us the nutrients our bodies need to function properly. What we desire and put action into is what we will receive or reap the proceeds of. If we show more love and kindness toward those around us, we will receive back to us the same emotions—that is if the other person reciprocates the same feeling back.

Nature is very good at producing cause and effect in its existence. When a seed, under good conditions, drops to the ground, it will naturally grow into another plant of the same. When the dark clouds gather, the rain falls. When a dam is constructed across a stream, the stream is blocked from flowing any farther.

The scriptures, like the ones above, demonstrate this Cause and Effect law. Another verse that came to mind was the words about music, the voice of song "For my soul delighteth in the song of the heart; yea, the song of the righteous is a prayer unto me, and it shall be answered with a blessing upon their heads"(D&C 25:12). Sing with our hearts beautiful music and blessings will come. Heavenly tunes that touch our emotions always have a way of touching our spirit and bringing peace and delight to our day.

You will notice ghost towns where the main street structures wear the effects of time, which causes their gray warped wooden sides to falter and sway, eventually to collapse. Another good example of cause and effect is when one tediously takes the time and patience to line up a standing line of dominoes, one in front of the other, then at the planned time, or not, they fall, one right after the other till they are all resting back down on the table surface.

As far as society goes, the cause of contention, disagreement, or greed has the effect of countries or states going to war. Whereas, the effort to settle conflicts with understanding and fairness has the effect of peace and tolerance. The Universal Law of Cause and Effect is totally up to the individual to control and produce, depending on their desires and dreams. The Law of Compensation [23AR] is when the blessing, gifts, or money is distributed back to you as the result of the Law of Cause and Effect. We are compensated for our positive decisions and actions that we hope for and dream about, and for our time and effort and the value we have on our abilities.

Parable of Cause and Effect

Behold there was a rock that tumbled onto the road . . . that the walker tripped over . . . that spilled the contents of his seed bag, that caused the seeds to sink into the mud . . . that the sun shone on . . . that sprouted up . . . that blossomed . . . that produced seeds . . . that the seed man collected and put into his bag . . . that he sold at the market . . . that brought him a few coins . . . that bought him eyeglasses so he could see where he was going.

Photo credit: Michael-H-Photography via VisualHunt.com

> When we are no longer able
> to change a situation, we are
> challenged to change ourselves.
>
> —Victor Frankl, 1905–1997)

7. The Universal Law of Change.

This law is somewhat different in relationship to the Law of Cycles or Rhythms, which focuses more on to the phases of nature and man, in that we can apply it more to our personal lives than to anything else. If we are not pleased with how our lives are progressing, then we can make concise decisions to alter it into a different direction. We can change. If our circumstances or opportunities are not conducive to goodness or advancement, then we either need to change our attitude about how things are going or get into a better environment that supports improvements and a higher state of being. {24}

However, change can be challenging. It can be difficult. But it is never impossible. The Universal Law of Change, which just by its name implies, is a fact that gives anyone the opportunity to change from one state to another if they so desire. They just need to have faith and produce actions that accomplishes the transformation that is longed for. If I desire to transform my body to a physique that is more toned and firm, then with the dedicated effort, I can change my body to a healthier, fitter state. If I desire the ability to play the piano with grace and confidence, then I can change from inability to having a skilled talent by the same process of desire, persistent practice, and then enjoy the outcome of performing beautiful music for myself and others. Whatever we feel uncomfortable about, or lacking knowledge of, or just to be a little more skilled in something we enjoy, we can have the assurance that it is all possible using the Law of Change to get to where we want to be in character or abilities.

Repentance is part of the Law of Change. To make amends for the mistakes we have made using the amazing gift of grace through the atonement—because of the love of Jesus Christ—to lift the burden of sin from our hearts and minds and improve our spirits. To remove burdens of guilt and stress from our souls transforms one from distress and lowliness to one of light, forgiveness, and hope. Which also puts one on a much higher level of vibration and frequency with the positive spirit of love, peace, and joy (see # 21). Fixing what needs to be fixed within ourselves through prayer and courage. Only God changes not. He is alpha and omega, the beginning and the end; we are the ones that are here on earth to make our way back to Him through improving, learning, and changing. As Mormon 9:19 tells us, "And behold, I say unto you he changeth not; if so he would cease to be God; and he ceaseth not to be God, and is a God of miracles." We can eternally rely on our Lord to ever be consistent with all laws and blessings for our benefit because of His great love for us and encouraging us to change where need be to be our best and touch the lives of others in a most positive way.

No one is "stuck" in one place or in the same situation or thought permanently. It just doesn't happen. Change occurs if we like it or not. However, *how* we change is totally up to us, and how we think or how we look at things, for better or for worse. We can feel like we are "stuck in a rut," if that is how we believe we are thinking, and confirm that made-up "fact" to ourselves as an excuse to not do anything about changing our situation we are living in. It may seem like nothing changes; however, our mind either continues to digress in our thoughts or it improves with positive thinking. We attract what we think about most—which is the Law of Attraction (see Chapter 4).

Consequently, we need to be aware of what we see, what we listen to, how we speak, what kind of people we associate with, etc., to make desired changes in our lives. It is easier to be more spiritual and righteous around those who think the same—Law of Association and Fellowship (see Chapter 3 and 13)—than to be in a place that does not house that kind of individual, and so forth. We set goals at the beginning of each year, or try to, which means that we want to get better, to change, to progress, and to achieve. I think that we have an inherent desire to become better than we are. The Law of Change opens the door to the possibilities of our divine self evolving and accomplishing so much more—for ourselves, our family, and for the betterment of others.

Blessings or Consequences in the Scriptures for the Universal Law of Change

1. **Romans 12:2 –** <u>Transform</u> **= Renewing of Mind**
    "And be not conformed to this world; but be ye <u>transformed by</u> **the renewing of your mind, that ye may** <u>prove</u> **what is that good, and acceptable, and perfect, will of God."**

2. **1 Corinthians 15:51–52 –** <u>Changed</u> **– In a Twinkling of an Eye**
    Behold, I shew you a mystery; We shall not all sleep, but we shall all be changed.
    <u>In a moment, in the twinkling of an eye</u>**, at the last trump for the trumpet shall sound, and the dead shall be raised incorruptible, and we shall be changed.**

3. **Philippians 3:21 –** <u>Change Our Body</u> **– To Be Like God's**

    "Who shall <u>change our vile body,</u> that it may be fashioned like unto his glorious body, according to the working whereby he is able, even to subdue all things unto himself."

4. **Mosiah 5:7 –** <u>Hearts Changed</u> **= Become His Children**

    And now, because of the covenant which ye have made ye shall be called the children of Christ, his sons, and his daughters; for behold, this day he hath spiritually begotten you; for ye say that your <u>hearts are changed through faith on his name;</u> **therefore, ye are born of him and have become his sons and his daughters.**

5. **Alma 5:12–14 –** <u>Change of Heart</u> **= Spiritually Born of God**

    <u>And according to his faith</u> **there was a mighty change wrought in his heart, Behold I say unto you that this is all true. And behold, he preached the word unto your fathers, and a** <u>mighty change was also wrought in their hearts,</u> **and they** <u>humbled themselves and put their trust in the true and living God.</u> **And behold, they were faithful until the end; therefore they were saved. And now behold, I ask of you, my brethren of the church, have ye spiritually been born of God? Have ye received his image in your countenances? Have ye experienced this mighty change in your hearts?**

6. **3 Nephi 28:38–40** – <u>Bodies Changed</u> = **To Not Taste of Death**

    Therefore, that they might not taste of death <u>there was a change wrought upon their bodies,</u> that they might not suffer pain nor sorrow save it were for the sins of the world. Now this change was not equal to that which shall take place a the last day; but there was a <u>change wrought upon them,</u> insomuch that Satan could have no power over them, that he could not tempt them; and they were sanctified in the flesh, that they were holy, and that the powers of the earth could not hold them.

    And in this state they were to remain until the judgment day of Christ; and at that day they were to receive a greater change, and to be received into the kingdom of the Father to go no more out, but to dwell with God eternally in the heavens.

7. **Alma 19:6** – <u>Mind Changed</u> = **Received Light**

    Now, this was what Ammon desired, for he knew that king Lamoni was under the <u>power of God</u>; he knew that the dark veil of unbelief was being cast away from his mind, and the light which did light up his mind, which was the light of the glory of God, which was a marvelous light of his goodness- yea, this <u>light had infused such joy into his soul, the cloud of darkness having been dispelled, and that the light of everlasting life</u> was lit up in his soul, yea, he

knew that this had overcome his natural frame, and he was carried away in God.

8. D&C 9:8–9 – <u>Change of Feeling</u> = **Right or Wrong**
    But, behold, I say unto you, that you must <u>study it our in your mind; then you must ask me if it be right,</u> **and if it is right I will cause that your bosom shall burn within you; therefore, you shall feel that it is right. But if it be** <u>not right you shall have no such feelings</u>**, but you shall have a stupor of thought that shall cause you to forget the thing which is wrong; therefore, you cannot write that which is sacred save it be given you from me.**

9. Mosiah 27:10, 18–19, 23–24, 28–29 – <u>Change of Heart</u> = **Alma the Younger**
    And now it came to pass that while he was <u>going about to destroy the church of God,</u> **for he did go about secretly with the sons of Mosiah seeking to destroy the church, and** <u>to lead astray the people</u> **of the Lord, contrary to the commandments of God, or even the king. And now Alma and those that were with him** <u>fell again to the earth, for great was their astonishment; for with their own eyes they had behold an angel of the Lord;</u> **and his voice was as thunder, which shook the earth; and they knew that there was nothing save the power of God that could shake the earth and cause it to tremble as though it would part asunder. And now the** <u>astonishment of Alma was so great</u> **that he**

became dumb, that he could not open his mouth; yea, and he became weak, even that he could not move his hands; therefore he was taken by those that were with him, and carried helpless, even until he was laid before his father. And it came to pass after they had <u>fasted and prayed</u> for the space of two days and two nights, that limbs of Alma received their strength, and he stood up and began to speak unto them, bidding them to be of good comfort: For, said he, <u>I have repented of my sins</u> and have been redeemed of the Lord; behold I am born of the Spirit. Nevertheless, after <u>wading through much tribulation,</u> repenting nigh unto death, the Lord in mercy hath seen fit to snatch me out of an everlasting burning, and I am born of God. My soul hath been redeemed from the gall of bitterness and bonds of iniquity. I was in the darkest abyss; but now I behold the marvelous light of God. <u>My soul was racked with eternal torment;</u> but I am snatched, and my soul is pained no more.

10. **Helaman 15:7** – <u>Knowledge of Truth</u> = **Change of Heart**

And behold, ye do <u>know of yourselves, for ye have witnessed it,</u> that as many of them as are brought to the knowledge of the truth, and to <u>know of the wicked and abominable traditions of their fathers,</u> and are led to believe the holy scriptures, yea, the prophecies of the holy prophets, which are written, which <u>leadeth</u> them to faith

on the Lord, and <u>unto repentance</u>, **which faith
and repentance bringeth a change of heart unto
them.**

Summary

Change is a predictable constant. It takes place every hour
in every day. From changing beds to changing jobs. Change
comes without notice, or it occurs as a result of a well-thought-
out plan. The Law of Change deals mostly with individuals
rather than looking at the change of nature through the different phases of seasons or the comings and goings of present life ending and new life beginning—this law is more for
Cycles and Rhythms of the Universe of nature and man.

The ability to notice discontent or dissatisfaction in
our lives requires the thought of change to make it possible
to become better or feel more confident in ourselves. When
we become aware of our abilities and talents, we have the
divine competence born within us to achieve great things—
to reach our God-given potential. But first, change comes
within our hearts and minds. In order to get a different
frame of mind, we need to reprogram our out-of-date or
negative thinking. Change doesn't last without a new attitude or to recognize habits that are detrimental to progress
(see #24).

Repentance is a change of heart, a feeling of cleanli-
ness, and of losing a guilt burden. It changes one's levels
of being to a higher level of faith, goodness, and intelligence. The scriptures emphasize this for all mankind to fix
mistakes, ask for forgiveness of disobedience, and to come
closer to our divine selves and especially to God. Not taking
the effort to change ourselves keeps us dull, perhaps mov-

ing backward in progress and unfulfilled. True happiness in ourselves only comes through change and progression.

Parable of Change

Once there was a farmer who loved his land but dreamed of flying. "If I continue to plow my fields all day, I will never be able to feel the freedom like birds do," he said. So he sold his plow, changed his overalls, and went to where the planes were. He learned new skills and now freely flies high viewing the wonders of the fields below.

Photo credit: Prairiekittin via VisualHunt / CC BY-ND

There is great force hidden
in a gentle command.

—George Herbert, 1593–1633)

8. The Universal Law of Command.

Like a general leading his army that shouts commands for his troops to move forward here or there, we can do the same with our thoughts and minds that leads us in the direction that we desire to go. This is very similar to giving ourselves an affirmation, a statement of what we want or how to become. Something that we repeat daily, with conviction and emotion, to achieve a desired outcome. It is usually blunt and to the point, not a bunch of fancy words to stumble over, but a statement that is very clear and easy to picture and understand. [25AR]

The Universal Law of Command can either move you forward and be positive or it can backfire and negative results will manifest. Make sure you focus on what you want, not on what you don't want. To make the innocent statement of, "I usually catch a cold every winter," then there will be a big probability that it will happen because you unknowingly commanded it to yourself. Being aware of how you talk to yourself controls the commands your subconscious mind obeys. It doesn't know any better, it will follow or obey whatever you put into it as fact—be it good or bad. "Self-fulfilling prophesies" come through words that we just "throw out there" without thinking about them. Unintentional sentences or thoughts about ourselves or what we can or can't do. Thus saying "I can't" will manifest to you a never will, but if you say "I'll try" or "I can," then you most certainly will bring the possibility that it will happen.

Command statements or affirmations announce themselves frequently throughout the scriptures, especially from our Lord. He commanded the elements to form the heavens and the earth and to create mankind. They are matter-of-fact demands. No doubt involved in any way of their manifestation—complete faith and belief. {26} And that is the necessary ingredient to make our commands materialize as well—to believe and have no doubt about them coming. Picture what we want in your mind, speak affirmations, and command their existence as if you already have it. Do it continually until it actually appears or you transform into whatever you are visualizing for yourself.

Through belief, feeling, and action, results happen. So command to your subconscious what you want frequently throughout the day, and eventually, through your belief and actions, your dreams will come true.

Blessings or Consequences in the Scriptures for the Universal Law of Command

1. **Isaiah 55:11 –** <u>My Word</u> **– Accomplish What I Please**

    "**So shall** <u>my word be that goeth forth out of my mouth:</u> **it shall not return unto me void, but it shall accomplish that which I please, and it shall prosper in the thing whereto I sent it.**"

2. **Mark 11:23 –** <u>Say Without Doubt</u> **= Move Mountains**

    For verily I say unto you, That <u>whosoever shall say</u> **unto this mountain, Be thou removed, and be thou cast into the sea; and shall** <u>not doubt in his heart,</u> **but shall believe that those things which he saith shall come to pass; he shall have whatsoever he saith.**

3. **Genesis 1:3, 6, 9, 11, 14, 20, 24, 27 –** <u>And God Said</u> **= Earth and Life Creations**

    <u>And God said,</u> **Let there be light: and there was light.** <u>And God said,</u> **Let there be a firmament in the midst of the water, and let it divide the waters from the water.** <u>And God said,</u> **Let the waters under the heaven be gathered together**

into one place, and let the dry land appear: and it was so.

And God said, Let the earth bring forth grass, the herb yielding seed, and the fruit tree yielding fruit after his kind, whose seed is in itself, upon the earth: and it was so. And God said, Let there be lights in the firmament of the heaven to divide the day from the night; and let them be for signs, and for seasons, and for days, and years: And God said, Let the waters bring forth abundantly the moving creature that hath life, and fowl that my fly above the earth in the open firmament of heaven. And God said, Let the earth bring forth the living creature after his kind, cattle, and creeping thing, and beast of the earth after his kind: and it was so.

So God created man in his own image, in the image of God created he him; make and female created he them.

4. 1 Kings 17:4 – Commanded = Ravens To Feed
    "And it shall be, that thou shalt drink of the brook; and I have commanded the ravens to feed thee there."

5. Luke 8:25 – Command = Waters Obey
    "And he said unto them, Where is your faith? And they being afraid wondered, saying one to another, What manner of man is this! For he commandeth even the winds, and water, and they obey him."

6. 2 Corinthians 4:6 – <u>Commanded</u> – **Light to Shine**
    "For God, who <u>commanded the light</u> to shine <u>out of darkness,</u> hath shined in our hearts, to give the light of the knowledge of the glory of God in the face of Jesus Christ."

7. Exodus 14:21 – <u>Commanded</u> = **Sea Parted**
    "<u>And Moses stretched out his hand</u> over the sea; and the Lord caused the sea to go back by a strongest wind all that night, and made the sea dry land, and the waters were divided."

8. Isaiah 45:12 – <u>Commanded</u> = **The Heavens, Earth, and Man**
    "<u>I have made</u> the earth, and created man upon it: I, <u>even my hands, have</u> stretched out the heavens, and all their host <u>have I commanded.</u>"

9. Matthew 8:16 – <u>With Word</u> = **Cast Out Evil Spirits**
    "When the even was come, they brought unto him many that were possessed with devils: and he cast out the spirits <u>with his word,</u> and healed all that were sick:"

10. 1 Nephi 17:53–54 – <u>By Lord's Will</u> = **Shocked Brothers**
    And it came to pass that the Lord said unto me: <u>Stretch forth thine hand again</u> unto thy brethren, and they shall not wither before thee, but I will shock them, <u>saith the Lord,</u> and this

will I do, that they may know that I am the Lord their God. And it came to pass that I stretched forth my hand unto my brethren, and they did not wither before me; but the Lord did shake them, <u>even according to the word</u> **which he had spoken.**

Summary

The word *command* may seem overly harsh, but only if you put in into that arena of conflict, as in, "I command you to attack!" But if you use it to command thoughts for improvement or creation then putting the word into the focus of development, then that is a positive use of the word.

For self-improvement, we need to address our minds onto the field of imagery and affirmations in order to fulfill our dreams and righteous desires. Our thoughts have a way of dwelling on the negative of "what may go wrong," so concentrated effort is needed to command our thoughts to think the right thing, the positive vision and betterment of soul. [27AR]

Priesthood power also has the divine ability, with the power of God, to command certain actions or blessings. Prophets of old, as well as modern-day prophets, have the ability, following the will of God, to divide seas and cast out evil spirits. In fact, any worthy priesthood holder has the authority to command, through prayer, any proper and desired outcome upon the will of God. The creation of all things were organized and manifested through the command powers of our divine, eternal God. It was directly proclaimed, and it was so!

Affirmations are a type of command. When we want to reach a certain goal or manifest a better environment or situation or achievement, then persistently and religiously we need to say to ourselves—with feeling—words that tell our subconscious minds what to do or how to become' (see #24). For example: if I wanted more financial security, then I would say to myself a couple of times every day on a consistent basis, "I am wealthy!" "I have plenty of money for all my needs and wants!" By doing so, things will be attracted to you, or opportunities will develop that will bring your thoughts to reality.

"Ask, and it shall be given you." "Seek, and ye shall find." Even the Bible supports commands. And God created all things, "And God said, Let there be light: and there was light." He didn't say, "It would be nice if there was some light today, but maybe I'll wait until tomorrow to decide." When God makes up His mind, there is no debate, and things happen—for our benefit. Perhaps there are times when we need to be more precise and not procrastinate or be "wishy-washy" about a decision.

Commands are a definite decision. They are not a "well, let me think about it" kind of statement. They are sure, to the point, and committed. They make things happen. They progress forward ideas, thoughts, and desires. God gave us the ability to make decisions, and through His support of righteous thoughts, we can bring to pass great things for ourselves and those around us, by our command and commitment to correct, positive things.

Parable of Command

A certain city builder decided one day to move. "I will build a house in the country!" he declared. And so he bought the needed materials, placed them properly, poured, pounded, and did everything that was necessary. The materials obeyed what they were required to do under his leadership and abilities, and a fine new house was built.

Imagination is the beginning of
creation. You imagine what you desire,
you will what you imagine and at
last you create what you will.

—George Bernard Shaw, 1856–1950

9. The Universal Law of Creation/Gestation.

This law is the beginning of ideas and thoughts that create things. First we think of an idea, we see it in our mind's eye, we visualize it before it comes to pass in real life in a 3-D form, and then it is produced into reality. [28AR] All things that surround us or handy objects that we use every day were once originally formed in an investor's mind. Someone had a great idea, put it on paper, then made it come to pass as a real thing. It may take a certain amount of time to make this process complete, but with persistence, it will happen. This creative time element of creation is the Law of Gestation, {29} where an idea takes time to grow, takes a certain amount of time and effort to develop the plans for, and then to complete the production process to its final object outcome.

Some creation agendas may take millenniums of years to complete, in the case of our eternal Father in creating our magnificent world that we have the opportunity to dwell on. God formed just the right environment and resources for our comfortable existence to live on this special planet. God's imagination is quite amazing and truly appreciated and admired.

The Law of Creation is not only for things we touch, smell, and taste—which is quite a pleasure indeed, but it also encompasses the thoughts we create and our attitudes as well. If we think or create thoughts in our minds that sit and savor for a while and then are expressed in a negative way, then that conception of thought is not for our growth and benefit, but for our determent and shame.

Whereas creative impressions can take on the wonders of the imagination and bring about products of great use such as modern technology and use of nature's powers to fuel and give energies to better our homes and lives. Today's world has moved tremendously in inventions that would have boggled the mind a century ago. Imagination is unlimited, and thus we will witness far more advancements because of ideas, in our fast-moving future.

The Law of Creation is a law that resides in each of us. Everyone has the ability to dream, imagine, and create. For those who do and actually see it through to its manifestation are truly inventors indeed. Each of us, being God's children, have the divine skills born in us to imagine and bring forth great ideas for the betterment of ourselves and for all of mankind—to fulfill our purpose and mission by using the power of our minds and hearts to create a beautiful world for everyone.

Blessings or Consequences in the Scriptures for the Universal Law of Creation

1. **Genesis 1:1, 21, 25, 27** – Creation = **Heavens, Earth, Animals, Man**

    In the beginning God, created **the heaven and the earth. And** God created **great whales, and every living creature that moveth, which the waters brought forth abundantly, after their kind, and every winged fowl after his kind; and God saw that it was good.** And God made **the beast of the earth after his kind, and cattle after their kind, and everything that creepeth upon the earth after his kind; and God saw that it was good.** So God created **man in his own image, in the image of God created he him; male and female** created he them.

2. **Moses 3:5, 7** – Creation = **First Created Spiritually**

    And every plant of the field before it was in the earth, **and every herb of the field before it grew. For I, the Lord God,** created **all things, of which I have spoken,** spiritually, **before they**

were naturally upon the face of the earth. For I, the Lord God, had not caused it to rain upon the face of the earth. And I, the Lord God, had created all the children of men; and not yet a man to till the ground; for in heaven created I them; and there was not yet flesh upon the earth, neither in the water, neither in the air;

And I, the Lord God, formed man from the dust of the ground, and breathed into his nostrils the breath of life; and man became a living soul, the first flesh upon the earth, the first man also; nevertheless, <u>all things were before created</u>; but spiritually were they <u>created and made accordingly to my word</u>.

3.   Moses 7:30 – <u>Created</u> = Worlds without Number
      And were it possible that man could number the particles of the earth, yea, millions of earths like this, it would not be a beginning to the number of thy <u>creations;</u> and thy curtains are stretched out still; and yet thou art there, and thy bosom is there; and also thou art just; thou art merciful and kind forever;

4.   Ether 3:15 – <u>Created</u> = God's Image
      And never have I showed myself unto man whom <u>I have created</u>, for never has man believed in me as thou hast. Seest thou that ye are <u>created</u> after mine own image? Yea, even all men <u>were created in the beginning after mine own image</u>.

5. **1 Nephi 17:8** – <u>Build a Ship</u> = **Instructions from God**

   "**And it came to pass that the Lord spake unto me, saying: Thou shalt** <u>construct</u> **a ship,** <u>after the manner which I shall show thee,</u> **that I may carry thy people across these waters.**"

6. **D&C 29:31–32** – <u>Creation</u> = **Spiritual and Temporal**

   For <u>by the power of my Spirit created</u> **I them; yea, all things both spiritual and temporal. First spiritual, secondly temporal, which is the beginning of my work; and again, first temporal, and secondly spiritual, which is the last of my work.**

7. **D&C 88:17–20** – <u>Earth Created</u> = **For Celestial Bodies**

   And the redemption of the soul is through him that quickeneth all things, in whose bosom it is decreed that the poor and the meek of the earth shall inherit it. Therefore, it must needs be <u>sanctified from all unrighteousness, that it may be prepared</u> **for the celestial glory; For** <u>after it hath filled the measure of its creation,</u> **it shall be crowned with glory, even with the presence of God the Father;**

   That <u>bodies who are of the celestial</u> **kingdom may possess it forever and ever; for, for this intent was it** <u>made and created,</u> **and for this intent are they sanctified.**

8. **1 Nephi 16:10, 28–29** – <u>Created Liahona</u> = **Direction**

And it came to pass that as my father arose in the morning, and went forth to the tent door, to his great astonishment he behold <u>upon the ground</u> a round ball of curious workmanship; and it was of fine brass. And within the ball were two spindles; and the one <u>pointed</u> the way whither we should go into the wilderness. And it came to pass that I, Nephi, beheld the pointers which were in the ball, that they did work <u>according to the faith and diligence and heed</u> which we did give unto them. And there was also <u>written upon them</u> a new writing, which was plain to be read, which did give us understanding concerning the ways of the Lord; and it <u>was written</u> and <u>changed from time to time</u>, according to the faith and diligence which we gave unto it. And thus we see that <u>by small means</u> the Lord can bring about great things.

9. **1 Chronicles 22:5, 28:11–12** – <u>Build</u> = **Solomon's Temple**

2 Chronicles 5:1

And David said, Solomon my son is young and tender, and the house that is <u>to be builded</u> for the Lord must be exceeding magnifical, of fame and of glory throughout all countries . . . Then David <u>gave</u> to Solomon his son the pattern of the porch, and of the houses thereof, and of the treasuries thereof, and of the upper chambers thereof, and of the inner parlours thereof, and of the place of the mercy seat. And the pattern of all that he had by the spirit, of the courts of the house of the Lord, and of all the chambers round about, of the treasuries of the house of God, and of the treasuries of the dedicated things: Thus all the work that Solomon made for the house of the lord was finished: and Solomon brought in all the things that David his father had dedicated; and the silver, and the gold, and all the instruments, put he among the treasures of the house of God.

10. **Ether 2:16–17, 20 –** Build Barges = **Cross the Ocean**

And the Lord said; Go to work and build, after the manner of barges which ye have hitherto built. And it came to pass that the brother of Jared did go to work, and also his brethren, and built barges after the manner which they had built, according to the instructions of the Lord. And they were small, and they were light upon the water, even like unto the lightness of a fowl upon the water. And they were built after a manner that they were exceedingly tight, even that they would hold water like unto a dish; and the bottom thereof was tight like unto a dish; and the sides thereof were tight like unto a dish; and the end thereof were peaked; and the top thereof was tight like unto a dish; and the length thereof was the length of a tree; and

the door thereof, when it was shut, was tight like unto a dish. And the Lord said unto the brother of Jared: Behold, thou <u>shalt make</u> **a hole in the top, and also in the bottom: and then thou shalt suffer for air thou shalt unstop the hole and receive air. And if it be so that the water come in upon thee, behold, ye shall stop the hold, that ye may not perish in the flood.**

Summary

The Universal Law of Creation is an ability of thought that we all possess to the extent that we develop and use it. As children, we had a fantastic sense of imagination and fantasy which seems to fade as we got older, probably because we believed that it was not so necessary to pretend or create new ideas when the old ones work just fine, or it's a silly thing to sit and daydream. When it is the "daydreamers" that see beyond limitations and progress functions of man to exceed our exceptions, hopes, and dreams—to make the world a better place.

After all, we have traveled millions of miles through space to land on an unexplored moon, or created a device that you can hold in your hand that has the ability to connect with anybody of our choice around the world, or came up with the idea of cloning animals {30} and construct life-like robots {31} that can walk pretty much like any human being can and function just the same. Ideas in today's world seem to multiply and expand so fast that it is a little tricky to keep up with.

Even with all the amazing technology of today, it still does not compare to what God has done and created in our magnificent world and even within ourselves. We are forever discovering new, interesting, and exciting facts about nature and human abilities. All it takes is a need, an idea, an emotion, and then a production and result to create something tremendous or more compact to make our lives function a little better, to make them more fulfilling and easier, or perhaps just to have fun and express ourselves!

Parable of Creation/Gestation

Once there was a designer that wanted to build a stone fountain in the center of town. What do I want this fountain to look like and how will it display the water? the designer thought to himself. Soon the creator had lots of sketches drawn out to take to the city council for approval and to hire a stone layer. Day by day, the fountain began to shape into reality according to plan. Then the hour arrived when the beautiful fountain was complete, the many detailed drawing filed, and the designer was done with his project, and it was good.

Photo credit: Ian Sane via VisualHunt.com / CC BY

Man appears for a little while to laugh
and weep, to work and play, and then
to go to make room for those who shall
follow him in the never-ending cycle.

—Aiden Wilson Tozer, 1897–1963)

10. The Universal Law of Cycles and Rhythms.

For the Universal Law of Rhythms, I am throwing in the Universal Law of Cycles as well. Both of these two laws are very similar with only a slight difference between the two. The Law of Rhythms has to do with the ebb and flow of life's feelings and age phases of our time on earth. How the ocean tides gently wash onto the beach and then flow back out to sea, merging into other waves and then repeating the natural in and out process again and again. Or when you drop a stone into a pond of still water and watch the ripples form rings from the center to grow larger and larger and then finally disappear or fade away the farther they move away from the target. [32AR]

The Law of Cycles is a rise and fall in life. It is similar to a pendulum swing that sways from side to side, reaching its maximum thrust until it stops and immediately reverses its swing back to the other side, only to reach its high point and return. Sways in nature are not rushed but cycles back and forth gently and sometimes unnoticeable. Our feelings, our thoughts, and our actions seem to swing from one high or positive mood to something of a temporary negative state—happy, not so happy, doing great, then doing not so good. Nothing lasts. "This, too, shall pass" {33} is a familiar, appropriate phrase for this common cycle of feelings. Being aware of the Universal Law helps us "catch" the downtimes and keep them controlled knowing that the moment will pass and better emotions will return. It is also a time that teaches us to appreciate the better moments from the times that are not going our way, but realizing that happier times will come back. Rhythms is also the fact that nothing stays the same, change is always going to present itself, so we need to embrace change since it will also be constant—trying not to change is futile. If there is one constant, it is change.

Some refer to the Law of Rhythms as the Law of Cycles, which makes perfect sense since the two seem to talk about the same thing. The Law of Cycles is a coming and going movement too, such as the coming and going of the earth's cycles, from spring to summer on through to winter. The changing of the earth's weather cycles, as the coming up of the sun in the morning and the setting of the beautiful rays in the late afternoon. Life has its cycles as well. all living creatures come into the world as a newborn, then most live through their designed life's cycle, and as they reach the end of mortality, their bodies grow old, thus eventually passing away returning to Mother Earth again. Of course, as many people believe, our spirits carry on with life again in heaven. The cycles of nature carry through the same natural process of life—growing, living, and dying. Even the great heavenly globes of matter and fire that dwell in space delivers its functions and then burn out, only for new ones to develop and manifest—all in their own time, never pushing to be or become, just naturally evolving and creating.

The rise and fall of great empires and civilizations back through man's history goes through the same processes of the pendulum swing. Only the ones that hold on to righteousness and God are saved from destruction. Many people in the scriptures seem to maneuver from a few years of following God and happiness, only to fade, get caught up in pride and wickedness, then crash and burn—falling down to their destruction. Then generations after, people become righteous again. It seems that humankind is either one way or the other. But know this—one's life can hold on to Godliness all the way through with only temptations and moods to fight and get through only by holding on to Gods laws and love. We need to make our rhythms of habit positive and righteous.

Rhythms and Cycles are like dancing and music. The environment cycles through with the natural movement of cause, effect, and change, growing and dying. Man, who goes through the same process, also dwells among other humans from other cultures and countries who sing their own songs and play their own music, all different, yet all the same. Generations of people, social development, inventions and existence—humankind's music with unique notes to learn and pass on from each person to the next, a rhythm and cycle of itself.

Blessings or Consequences in the Scriptures for the Universal Law of Cycles and Rhythms

1. **4 Nephi 1:18, 24–26 –** <u>Righteous</u> **= Blessed, to Unrighteous = Divisions**

    And how <u>blessed</u> **were they! For the Lord did** <u>bless</u> **them in all their doings; yea, even they** <u>were blessed</u> **and prospered until an hundred and ten years had passed away; and the first generation from Christ had passed away, and there was no contention in all the land. And now, in this two hundred and first year there began to be among them those** <u>who were lifted up in pride,</u> **such as the** <u>wearing of costly apparel,</u> **and all manner of fine pearls, and of the fine things of the world. And** <u>from that time forth</u> **they** <u>did have their goods and their substance no more common among them.</u> **And they** <u>began to be divided into classes</u>**; and they** <u>began to build up churches</u> **unto themselves to get gain, and** <u>began to deny the true church of Christ.</u>

2. **1 Nephi 16:4–5, 18 –** Nephi's Brethren in and out of righteousness **= When righteous, hope.**

   And it came to pass that I, Nephi, did exhort **my brethren, with all diligence, to** keep the commandments of the Lord. **And it came to pass that they did** humble themselves **before the Lord; insomuch that I had joy and great hopes of them, that they would walk in the paths of righteousness,**

   And it came to pass that I, Nephi, did speak much unto my brethren, **because they had hardened their hearts again, even unto complaining against the Lord their God.**

3. **1 Nephi 17:17–18, 47, 54–55 –** Nephi's Brethren From Murmuring to Worship **= Back to the Lord**

   And when my brethren saw that I was about to build a ship, they began to murmur **against me, saying: Our brother is a fool, for he thinketh that he can build a ship; yea, and he also thinketh that he can cross these great waters. And thus my brethren** did complain against me, **and were desirous that they might not labor, for they** did not believe that I could **build a ship; neither would they believe that I was instructed of the Lord. Behold, my soul is rent with anguish because of you, and my heart is pained; I fear lest ye shall be cast off forever. Behold, I am full of the Spirit of God, insomuch that my frame has no strength. And it came to pass that** I stretched forth my hand **unto my brethren, and**

they did not wither before me; but the Lord did shake them, even according to the word which he had spoken. And now, they said: We know of a surety that the Lord is with thee, for we know that it is the power of the Lord that has shaken us. And they fell down before me, and were about to worship me, but I would not suffer them, saying: I am thy brother, yea, even thy younger brother; therefore, worship the Lord thy God, and honor thy father and they mother, that thy days may be long in the land which the Lord thy God shall give thee.

4. **D&C 59:18–19** – Earth in Season = **Gladden the Heart**

    Yea, all things which come of the earth, in the season thereof, are made for the benefit and the use of man, both to please the eye and to gladden the heart:

    Yea, for food and for raiment, for taste and for smell, to strengthen the body and to enliven the soul.

5. **D&C 88:42–45** – Times and Seasons = **Creation Order**

    And again, verily I say unto you, he hath given a law unto all things, by which they move in their times and their seasons; And their courses are fixed, even the courses of the heavens, and the earth, which comprehend the earth and all the planets. And they give light to each other in their times and in their season, in their min-utes, in their hours, in their days, in their weeks, in their months, in their years—**all these are one year with God, but not with Man. The earth** rolls upon her wings **and the sun** giveth his light by day, **and the moon** giveth her light by night, **and the stars also** give their light, **as they roll upon their wings in their glory, in the midst of the power of God.**

6. **D&C 89:11** – Food in Season = **Health and Gratitude**

"**Every herb** in the season thereof, **and every fruit** in the season thereof; **all these to be used with prudence and thanksgiving.**"

7. **D&C 64:32** – Time = **Come to Pass**

"**But all things** must come to pass in their time."

8. **D&C 121:31** – Times and Revolutions = **Revealed in Fullness of Time**

All the times **of their** revolutions, all the appointed days, months, and years, and all the days of their days, months, and years, and all their glories, laws, and set times, **shall be revealed in the days of the dispensation of the fullness of times.**

9. **Abraham 3:4** – Kolob = **Lord's Time**

And the Lord said unto me, by the Urim and Thummim, that Kolob was after the manner of

the Lord, <u>according to its times and seasons in the</u> <u>revolutions</u> **thereof; that** <u>one revolution was a day</u> <u>unto the Lord</u>, **after his manner of reckoning,** <u>it</u> <u>being one thousand years</u> **according to the time appointed unto that whereon thou standest, This is the reckoning of the Lord's time,** <u>accord-</u> <u>ing to the reckoning</u> **of Kolob.**

10. **Ecclesiastes 3:1–8 –** <u>Time</u> **= To Accomplish Everything**

    To every thing there is a season, and a time <u>to every purpose</u> **under the heaven: A time** <u>to be</u> <u>born,</u> **and a time** <u>to die;</u> **a time** <u>to plant,</u> **and a time** <u>to pluck up</u> **that which is planted: A time** <u>to kill,</u> **and a time** <u>to heal;</u> **a time** <u>to break down,</u> **and a time** <u>to build up;</u> **A time** <u>to weep,</u> **and a time** <u>to laugh;</u> **a time** <u>to mourn,</u> **and a time** <u>to dance;</u> **A time** <u>to cast away stones,</u> **and a time** <u>to gather</u> <u>stones together;</u> **a time** <u>to embrace,</u> **and a time** <u>to</u> <u>refrain from embracing;</u> **A time** <u>to get,</u> **and a time** <u>to lose;</u> **a time** <u>to keep,</u> **and a time** <u>to cast away;</u> **A time** <u>to rend,</u> **and a time** <u>to sew;</u> **a time** <u>to keep</u> <u>silence,</u> **and a time** <u>to speak;</u> **A time** <u>to love,</u> **and a time** <u>to hate;</u> **a time** <u>of war,</u> **and a time** <u>of peace.</u>

Summary

As the rhythm of time cycles around, it has a way of repeating itself or the ideas that manifest in that time. At least with the styles of interior design, it is said that "if you don't like the style, just wait a few years and it will come back again."

Life has its programmed eternal beauty and purpose. All living things, both man and beast, are born, live in purpose or survival, then die, only to rise again in the hereafter. Round and round are humans brought to life, pass on, then more of us are brought from the premortal life to start a new physical one. {34} The phases of life can be like a dance that is strung out through the years of living. The excitement and curiously of youth, through the joys and challenges of learning and family, on to the purpose-filled, self-improvement, sharing end of life—cycling through both joy and sorrows.

Just being aware of our own rhythms and cycles of mood and feelings will help ease the comfortableness of changing from one end of the pendulum swing to the next. It is a natural and constant sensation. It helps to form appreciation for the happiness of heart from the mediocre feelings of "so-so" or "not-so-good." Focusing on the beautiful creations of nature soothes our hearts and souls. Watching the smooth, rhythmic ups and downs of a graceful bird on the wing as it glides through the air or soaking in the hypnotic washing of constant, cleansing waves as they almost silently flow upon the sandy beach and back again. The Universal Law of Cycles and the Universal Law of Rhythms are heaven's gift to mankind—for himself and God's earthly creations.

The Universal Law of Cycles and Rhythms also reminds us that nothing stays the same. Everything on earth has a beginning and an ending, with flows and ebbs in between. Nature has its lifespan just like man and animals do, from spring to summer, through fall ending with winter, and then starting all over again, from birth to death. Even though stages of life play their part, they are beautiful. Each moment, or hour, or day, or year we are alive, we have the opportunity to learn, to grow, to develop, and to share.

Our testimony also has its times of weakness and of strength as we go through trials in our lives. Unexpected situations that arise test our faith, which, when dwelt with properly handling the hardship with the right attitude and prayer, will progress us stronger in our commitment and covenants, thus receiving more strength and blessings.

Even our everyday duties have their comings and goings—get up, go to work, or get the family ready for school, do daily chores, welcome home children from school, come home from work, get supper, be together for a while with homework, etc., then off to bed to hear the alarm clock telling us to get up and repeat it all once again. It may sound monotonous; however, each moment is precious, and each day can be a treasure with the people that we love and witness our lives with.

There is always enough and an appropriate time to accomplish the things we desire in life. As the above scripture teaches, "A time to laugh, a time to love, a time to sow, a time to reap," and I might add, a time to create, a time to manifest our dreams, and a time to achieve anything we desire and work for!

Parable of Cycles and Rhythms

In a young neighborhood, there was a new house with a beginning family residing therein. In a few years, the paint on the not-so-new house needed painting, and the fence needed repair. The family children were older, and they all could work together fixing things that needed to be up-to-date. Soon some of the members of the family lived somewhere else, and the house became too large. Eventually, everyone moved away to different towns and smaller places. The neighborhood became aged but stable, then another young family moved in.

Photo credit: Natalia Medd via VisualHunt / CC BY

Quantum physics thus reveals a
basic oneness of the universe.

—Erwin Schrodinger, 1887–1961

11. The Universal Law of Divine Oneness/Energy.

Divine Oneness teaches us that we are all connected in energies and soul. Everything in the universe, including our world and all the living and breathing of life upon it— being from nature, animals, or human beings are all connected to the same energies that created us. We may be on different frequencies and existing on different vibrations, but we all embrace the divine God who created us. We are all one because we are intertwined with the same substance that formed us. [35AR]

When we go on a mountainous hike or a stroll through a flowering meadow, do we not "feel" the energy that radiates from the ground and plants that surrounds us? And do we not "soak in" the spiritual aura that illuminates from their divine formation? We are connected with them and them to us. We "feed" off of each other's vibrations and energies, which rejuvenate and lights our souls.

Because all of God's children—which we are—come from Him and from our home on high. As spirit children with Him, we have all come to earth with His divine greatness in us. We all have the same spiritual light within our hearts that gives us strength and hope if we choose to let it be so. We can connect with each other with our spirits, with our eternal concerns and love. None of us are alone. We may not see our "oneness," but we can feel it if we pay attention and realize that we are all on this earth with the same purpose and ability to return back to our heavenly home. It does not matter if we are different, if we live in different locations on earth, or if our skin is another color and we speak a different language, we are all God's children, and we all are connected because of the Plan of Salvation, as well as by the energies that surround ourselves and the natural living earth.

Because we are all "one," we can help each other and have charity one with another.

The feelings we have for someone in need, for someone who is having a tough time or is struggling inside. We have this natural tendency to assist others who are down and need help getting back up, to get them steady and going again. This "Oneness" touches heart to heart without reservation or discrimination, a unity develops because of this

Universal Law. Only those who have hardened this feeling have opposite tendencies.

The earth and everything on it was created by our loving Heavenly Father from the dust and the elements to form a world and to form mankind to be like Himself, in His own image, with His greatness, thus making everything existing flowing together connected by Divine Oneness.

Blessings or Consequences in the Scriptures for the Universal Law of Divine Oneness/Energy.

1. **D&C 88:41 – <u>God</u> = Through All Things**

   He <u>comprehendeth all things, and all things are before him</u>, **and** <u>all things are round about him; and he is above all things, and in all things, and is through all things</u>, **and** <u>is round about all things; and all things are by him</u>, **and of him, even God, forever and ever.**

2. **4 Nephi 1:13, 15–18 – <u>People Oneness of Heart</u> = Peace and Blessings**

   And it came to pass that there was <u>no contention</u> **among all the people, in all the land; but there were** <u>might miracles wrought</u> **among the disciples of Jesus. And it came to pass that there was no contention in the land, because of the** <u>love of God which did dwell in the hearts </u>**of the people.**

   And there were <u>no envyings, nor strifes, nor tumults, nor whoredoms, nor lyings, nor murders, nor any manner of lasciviousness;</u> **and surely there could not be a happier people among all**

the people who had been created by the hand of God. There were no robbers, nor murderers, neither were there Lamanites, nor any manner of -ites; but they were in one, the children of Christ, and hears to the kingdom of God. And how blessed were they! For the Lord did bless them in all their doings; yea, even they were blessed and prospered until an hundred and ten years had passed away; and the first generation from Christ had passed away, and there was no contention in all the land.

3. **4 Nephi 1:3** – Everyone = **Equal**
    "**And they had** all things common among them; **therefore there were** not rich and poor, bond and free, **but they were** all made free, **and partakers of the heavenly gift.**"

4. **Alma 40:11** – All People = **Spirit's Return to God.**
    Behold, it has been made known unto me by an angel, that the spirits **of all men, as soon as they are departed from this mortal body, yea, the** spirits **of all men, whether they** be good or evil, **are** taken home **to that God who gave them life.**

5. **Ether 3:15–16** – All Mankind = **After God's Image**
    Yea, even all men **were created in the beginning after mine own image. Behold, this body, which ye now behold, is the body of my spirit;**

and man have I <u>created after the body of my spirit</u>; and even as I appear unto thee to be in the spirit will I appear unto my people in the flesh.

6. **D&C 88:15** – <u>Spirit and Body</u> = **Soul of Man**
   "And the <u>spirit and the body</u> are the soul of man."

7. **Psalms 82:6** – <u>All Mankind</u> = **Children of God.**
   "I have said, Ye are gods; and <u>all of you are children</u> of the most High."

8. **D&C 93:29, 33, 35, 38** – <u>Mankind</u> = **In the Beginning With God**
   <u>Man</u> was also in the beginning with God. <u>Intelligence,</u> or the light of truth, was not created or made, neither indeed can be. <u>For man is spirit.</u> The elements are eternal, and <u>spirit and element, inseparably connected</u>, receive a fullness of joy; <u>The elements</u> are the tabernacle of God; yea, man is the tabernacle of God, even temples; and whatsoever temple is defiled, God shall destroy that temple. <u>Every spirit of man</u> was innocent in the beginning; and God having redeemed man from the fall, <u>men became again,</u> in their infant state, innocent before God.

9. **D&C 121:45–46** – <u>All Mankind</u> = **Give Charity**
   <u>Let thy bowels</u> also be full of charity towards all men, and to the household of faith, and let virtue garnish <u>thy thoughts</u> unceasingly; then

shall thy confidence wax strong in the presence of God; and the doctrine of the priesthood shall distill upon thy soul as the dews from Heaven. The Holy Ghost shall be thy constant companion, and thy scepter an unchanging scepter of righteousness and truth; and thy dominion shall be an everlasting dominion, and without compulsory means it shall flow unto thee forever and ever.

10. Moses 3:7 – All Mankind – Created From the Dust of the Earth

"And I, the Lord God, formed man from the dust of the ground, and breathed unto his nostrils the breath of life; and man became a living soul, the first flesh upon the earth, the first man also . . ."

Summary

The universe and all that are in that sphere are connected by energies that make everything as "one." We all have a vibrating aura that surrounds us and touches all that we are in connection with, including the earth that we stand on and to each other. {36} When we "ground" or stand in soft soils or soothing sands with our bare feet, we gather the power and energies from the earth into our bodies, which balances our own energies for a more healthier state. {37}

The Universal Law of Oneness encompasses everything. We are created from the earth by our divine Father, and we will return to the earth when we pass away. The variety of animals, plants, trees, rocks, fish, and fowl all carry the same elements of origin as mankind does. In the beginning, God created the heavens and the earth and all living things from Universal Laws that demanded their use in order to fill the magnificent order.

We have God's power and ability to create and love in all of us. We are "one" in the fact that we all have divine powers to find, develop, and share. We were born on earth not knowing our potential, but when acknowledged, we accomplish great and worthwhile things.

God's spirit and light are around us and through us from moment to moment, from season to season, from birth to death. We are all spiritual brothers and sisters no matter where we are lodging on the planet. We all have different ways of doing things, of beliefs, of cultures, of dress, or even of how we eat, but we don't have to be the same to be one. Not only are the energies from living creatures and plants connected to us, but the fact that we are all humans experiencing mortality that makes us as "one."

Parable of Divine Oneness/Energy

There once was a baker who was making a batch of cookies. The ingredients were of high quality and purchased from the purest of sources. Adding each ingredient from the flour to the eggs, the dough was perfect and sweet. Rolling out the dough onto the primed wooden surface, the baker meticulously cut out each round cookie, all the same shape and deliciousness. However, during the cooking process, each cookie formed very slightly a little differently; nonetheless, they all came from the same cookie batch with heavenly ingredients—as with us.

Photo credit: Paxson Woelber via Visual Hunt / CC BY

Faith is to believe what we do not
see, and the reward of this faith
is to see what we believe.

—Saint Augustine, 354–430)

12. The Universal Law of Faith.

Anything that we look forward to that we cannot see requires an attitude of faith. Faith is what holds most all the other laws up for completion. We need to believe and have a strong foundation of faith that what we dream of will manifest itself through all of our concerns or insufficient degree of knowledge. It makes the impossible possible. Faith is what miracles are made of. The Universal Law of Faith has a high vibration that mixes with the light of the divine. It is through faith that miracles and great happenings came to pass in the scriptures. Through our prayers, we communicate with our Heavenly Father. Even though we do not physically see Him, we have tender faith that He hears our pleas and thanksgivings. [38AR]

Not only does it take faith to believe in our heavenly Savior, but it takes faith within ourselves and our abilities to accomplish goals we have set for ourselves, or just to have faith in ourselves to give a presentation, a talk, or perform for an audience. Faith means constantly listening to and abiding by our intuition and inner guidance. When we have faith, we handle fear easily and with confidence. Both fear and faith are feelings that are generated from a source unseen, we do not see what is ahead, so choose faith over fear. When we have sufficient faith, we can turn our struggles or hopes to the divine for His strength, thus we put our total trust in Him and our own abilities that we were blessed with. Take that first step in the unseen future, the dark tunnel of uncertainty, and have faith that the Lord will direct you toward what is best for you in your life. You don't have to see the end of the ladder before you step up and stand on the first step going up. Sometimes you just figure it out as you go with the Lord taking your hand. If you don't move, you have no faith.

The acts of faith revolves daily around us. We trust or have faith that the sun will rise in the east at the right time each morning and that it will sink down below the darkening horizon every evening. We have faith that other Universal Laws will be dependable and unchangeable. That when we apply them in our living, the positive outcome through obeying them will be delivered to us without any doubt of their blessings. Blessings also come from having faith in priesthood power and in the brethren's worthiness to perform necessary blessings. Many miracles of tender healings performed by those who had the authority to return sight to the blind or the ability to walk, after parts of a lifetime of yearning to do so. Jesus Christ himself, the master healer, plus other priesthood bearers through ages past, as well as those of today have blessed many through the faith of those transformed.

Faith is to consistently believe in our positive thoughts or dreams to come into being through humble reliance for our goodness from our Lord. FAITH = For Anyone can Invariably Trust in Him. Have faith through righteously obeying the Universal Laws and the Laws of God. That you will receive all the deserved blessings that await you because of your faithfulness.

Blessings or Consequences in the Scriptures for the Universal Law of Faith

1. **Enos 1:8** – Never Seen = **Became Whole**
   And he said unto me: Because of thy faith in Christ, **whom thou hast** never before heard nor seen**. And many years pass away before he shall manifest himself in the flesh; wherefore, go to, thy faith hath made thee whole.**

2. **Hebrews 11:1** – Faith = **Hoped For Not Seen**
   "Now faith **is the substance of things hoped for, the evidence of things not see."**

3. **James 1:5–6** – <u>Ask in Faith</u> = **Receive Knowledge**
   If any of <u>you lack wisdom, let him ask of God,</u> **that giveth to all men liberally, and upbraideth not; and it shall be given him. But let** <u>him ask in faith, nothing wavering.</u> **For he that wavereth is like a wave of the sea driven with the wind and tossed.**

4. **D&C 29:6** – <u>Ask in Faith</u> = **Receive**
   "And, as it is written – <u>Whatsoever ye shall ask in faith,</u> **being united in prayer according to my command, ye shall receive."**

5. **Moses 7:13** – <u>Great Faith</u> = **Great Commands**
   <u>And so great was the faith</u> **of Enoch that he led the people of God, and their enemies came to battle against them; and he spake the word of the Lord, and the earth trembled, and the mountains fled, even according to his command; and the rivers of water were turned out of their course; and the roar of the lions was heard out of the wilderness; and all nations feared greatly, so powerful was the word of Enoch, and so great was the power of the language which God had given him.**

6. **Moroni 10:4** – <u>Ask in Faith</u> = **Receive Answer**
   And when ye shall receive these things, I would exhort you that ye would <u>ask God, the Eternal Father, in the name of Christ, if these things are not true; and if ye shall ask with a sincere heart, with real intent, having faith in Christ,</u>

he will manifest the truth of it unto you, by the power of the Holy Ghost.

7. Matthew 21:21–22 – <u>Faith, Doubt Not</u> = Received

    Jesus answered and said unto them, verily I say unto you, <u>If ye have faith, and doubt not, ye</u> shall not only do this which is done to the fig tree, but also if ye shall say unto this mountain, Be thou removed, and be thou cast into the sea; it shall be done. And all things, whatsoever <u>ye shall ask in prayer, believing,</u> ye shall receive.

8. 1 Nephi 4:5–7 – <u>Faith Not Knowing</u> = Lead By The Spirit

    "I, Nephi, crept into the city and went forth towards the house of Laban." "And I was <u>led by the Spirit, not knowing beforehand the things which I should do.</u>' "Nevertheless I went forth, . . ."

9. Matthew 9:22 – <u>Faith</u> = Made Whole

    "But Jesus turned him about, and when he saw her, he said, Daughter, be of good comfort; <u>thy faith</u> hath made thee whole. And the woman was made whole from that hour."

10. D&C 8:10 – <u>Without Faith</u> = Can Do Nothing

    "Remember that <u>without faith</u> you can do nothing; <u>therefore ask in faith.</u> Trifle not with these things; do not ask for that which you ought not."

Summary

It takes a certain amount of faith to move forward into uncertain areas especially when we cannot see the definite end result, but then that is what faith is all about. Isn't it? The Universal Law of Faith is the foundation of the fulfillment of many of the Universal Laws, especially the Spiritual Laws. The Universal Law of Belief or the Law of Command, for instance, requires an amount of faith in order to reap their benefits.

A great amount of confidence and faith helps us achieve set goals and visualized dreams. It puts motivation into our hearts that keeps us moving forward with our creative ideas or thoughts, even though they are still in the manifestation stage. We trust and have faith that things will work out for our best good. We have faith that our most sought-after desires will come true with God's help and the hard effort we put into achieving them. Faith in ourselves and our abilities to accomplish what we want no matter how we feel. Courage in spite of fear. Hope instead of doubt. Faith to step forward trusting in our instincts and in God's guidance.

Faith is everywhere in our everyday. Faith that the car will start. Faith that it will rain when the ground is dry from the summer sun. Even faith in others that have the power to give us blessings or to just give us support and encouragement—that our family and good friends will just be there for us. But most of all, faith that God is real and that He loves us now and forever and is always aware of who we are and what our needs are. We may not know exactly which road to take or which career to train for, but through study, making the best decision that we can, pray about it and then move ahead with faith that all will be well and great things will happen in our lives.

Parable of Faith

Once upon a time, there was a worker who was needed no longer at his job. "What will I do now?" the worker said. "I will search for another position." Day after day, from one business to another, he inquired. I will learn more and do the best that I can . . . it will be okay, the worker thought to himself, after finding no openings—as yet. "I will not give up, and I will keep trying," declared the worker. "I will find something that is just for me." At the right time, the worker found the best work that he had ever had! Once upon a time, the worker knew, eventually, that things would work out.

Photo credit: EarthDayPictures via Visualhunt / CC BY

We must cherish one another, watch
over one another, comfort one another,
and gain instruction that we may
all sit down in heaven together.

—Lucy Mack Smith, 1775–1856

13. Universal Law of Fellowship.

When two or more individuals with the same idea or purpose in mind gather together to center with that idea,
then the Universal Law of Fellowship is formed. Groups
that assemble together to support each other in the same
belief or idea carries an energy or a connection that produces stronger vibrations between members. Similar to

attending church on Sunday. Members who congregate together receive spiritual strength not only from the energy produced from a crowd, but also the opportunity to add your righteous thoughts to help rise others more to a divine state. [39AR]

Of course, the Law of Fellowship applies to any kind of a gathering, be it of good purpose or not, that has the same idea in mind. This goes for people that form together to fight or riot against other people, government actions, or cultural differences. More positive actions of groups with the same purpose could entail environmental support groups or those with the same ideas to clean up oceans or save endangered species.

Off and on throughout the scriptures, people have gathered in groups for righteous support or for Gadianton types of disturbance. {40} The most significant biblical gathering was the sermon on the mount, the feeding of the five thousand, or from the Book of Mormon, the visit from Jesus to the Nephites (see below). The history of the early saints provide a picture of fellowshipping when they gathered and walked across the plains to settle in Utah. {41} They believed in the same God, they had the same faith, and they had the same desire to service God and move their families to an area where settlements could establish themselves and flourish.

The Law of Fellowship brings people together for a specific or universal cause. Hopefully for a gathering that supports righteous endeavors and helps move progress forward in a peaceful, unified way or enriches people's hearts toward God, faith, service, and joy. Assembling individuals with the same belief or idea can bring a stronger spirit or vibration to the gathering which carries a positive energy among its members. However, grouping as people with negative ill purpose in mind can carry a very dangerous force with it. As with any of the other laws, obeying laws and following after righteousness will always bring positive groups together that will only bring good will and peace to the multitude and society.

Blessings or Consequences in the Scriptures for the Universal Law of Fellowship

1. **3 Nephi 11:1, 8** – <u>Nephite Gathering</u> – **To Witness Jesus Christ**
    And now it came to pass that there were a <u>great multitude gathered together,</u> **of the people of Nephi**, **round about the temple which was in the land. Bountiful; and they were marveling and wondering one with another, and were showing one to another, the great and marvelous change which had taken place. And it came to pass,** <u>as they understood they cast their eyes up again towards heaven;</u> **and behold, they saw a Man descending out of heaven; and he was clothed in a white robe; and he came down and stood in the midst of them; and the** <u>eyes of the whole multitude were turned upon him,</u> **and they durst not open their mouths, even one to another, and wist not what it meant, for they thought it was an angel that had appeared unto them.**

2. **Matthew 5:1, 7:28–29, 8:1** – Multitude = **Jesus Taught**

   And seeing the multitudes, **he went up into a mountain: and** when he was set, his disciples came unto him: **And it came to pass, when Jesus had ended these sayings, the people were astonished at his doctrine: For he taught them as one having authority, and not as the scribes. When he was come down from the mountain, great multitudes followed him.**

3. **Matthew 14:13–14, 19–20** – Multitude Gathered = **Jesus Taught and Feed**

   When Jesus heard of it, he departed thence by ship into a desert place apart; and when the people had heard thereof, they followed him **on foot out of the cities. And Jesus went forth, and** saw a great multitude, **and was moved with** compassion toward them, and he healed their sick. And he commanded the multitude **to sit down on the grass, and took the five loaves, and the two fishes, and looking up to heaven, he blessed, and brake, and gave the loaves to his disciples, and the disciples to the multitude. And** they did all eat, and were filled: **and they took up of the fragments that remained twelve baskets full.**

4. 1 Nephi 11:33–36 – <u>Multitudes Against Jesus</u> = **Great the Fall Thereof**

    And I, Nephi, saw that he was lifted up upon the cross and slain for the sins of the world. And after he was slain I saw the <u>multitudes of the earth, that they were gathered together to fight against the apostles of the Lamb</u>; for thus were the twelve called by the angel of the Lord. And the <u>multitude of the earth was gathered together;</u> and I behold that they were in a large and spacious building, like unto the building which my father saw. And the angel of the Lord spake unto me again, saying: <u>Behold the world </u>and the wisdom thereof; yea, <u>behold the house of Israel hath gathered together to fight </u>against the twelve apostles of the Lamb. And it came to pass that I saw and bear record, that the great and spacious building was the pride of the world; and it fell, and the fall thereof was exceedingly great. And the angel of the Lord spake unto me again, saying: Thus shall be the destruction of all nations, kindreds, tongues, and people, that shall fight against the twelve apostles of the Lamb.

5. 3 Nephi 11:12, 14–17 – <u>Multitude </u>= **Worshiped Jesus**

    And it came to pass that when Jesus had spoken these words the <u>whole multitude fell to the earth;</u> for they remembered that it had been prophesied among them that Christ should show himself unto them after his ascension into heaven. **Arise and come forth unto me, that ye may thrust your hands into my side, and also that ye may feel the prints of the nails in my hands and in my feet, that ye may know that I am the God of Israel, and the God of the whole earth, and have been slain for the sins of the world. And it came to pass that the** multitude went forth, and thrust their hands into his side, and did feel the prints of the nails in his hands and in his feet; and this they did do, going forth one by one until they had all gone forth, and did see with their eyes and did feel with their hands, and did know of a surety **and did bear record, that it was he, of whom it was written by the prophets, that should come. And** when they had all gone forth and had witnessed **for themselves,** they did cry out with one accord, **saying: Hosanna! Blessed by the name of the Most High God! And** they did fall down at the feet of Jesus, and did worship him.

6. **Matthew 12:15 –** Multitudes Followed **= Jesus Healed**

   "But when Jesus knew it, he withdrew himself from thence: and great multitudes followed him, **and he healed them all;"**

7. **Mosiah 18:7–8, 10–11, 16–17 –** Believers of Alma **= Baptized in the Waters of Mormon**

   And it came to pass after many days there were a goodly number gathered together **at the**

place of Mormon, to hear the words of Alma. Yea, all were <u>gathered together that believed on his word, to hear him.</u> And he did teach them, and did preach unto them repentance, and redemption, and faith on the Lord. And it came to pass that he said unto them: Behold, here are the waters of Mormon (for thus were they called) and now, as ye are <u>desirous to come into the fold of God, and to be called his people, and are willing to bear one another's burdens,</u> that they may be light;

Now I say unto you, if this be the desire of your hearts, what have you against being baptized in the name of the Lord, as a witness before him that ye have entered into a covenant with him, that ye will serve him and keep his commandments, that he may pour out his Spirit more abundantly upon you? And now <u>when the people had heard these words, they clapped their hands</u> for joy and exclaimed: <u>This is the desire of our hearts.</u> And after this manner he did baptize every one that went forth to the place of Mormon; and they were in number about two hundred and four souls; yea, and they were baptized in the waters of Mormon, and were filled with the grace of God.

And they were called the church of God, or the church of Christ, from that time forward. And it came to pass that whosoever was baptized by the power and authority of God was added to his church.

8. **2 Nephi 5:6–-10 – <u>Nephi's People</u> = Gather To Follow God**

    Wherefore, it came to pass that <u>I, Nephi, did take my family, and also Zoram</u> and his family, and Sam, mine elder brother and his family, and Jacob and Joseph, my younger brethren, and also my sisters, and <u>all those who would go with me. And all those who would go with me</u> were those who believed in the warnings and the revelations of God; wherefore, they did hearken unto my words. And we did take our tents and whatsoever things were possible for us, and did journey in the wilderness for the space of many days. And after we had journeyed for the space of many days we did pitch our tents.

    <u>And my people</u> would that we should call the name of the place Nephi; wherefore, we did call it Nephi. And <u>all those who were with me</u> did take upon them to call themselves the people of Nephi. And we did observe to keep the judgments, and the statutes, and the commandments of the Lord in all things, according to the law of Moses.

9. **Matthew 18:20 – <u>Two or Three</u> – In My Name**
    "For where <u>two or three are gathered together in my name,</u> there am I in the midst of them."

10. **D&C 63:36 – <u>Saints of God</u> = Assemble Together**
    "Wherefore, seeing that I, the Lord, have decreed all these things upon the face of the earth, I will that <u>my saints</u> should be assembled upon the land of Zion;"

Summary

People with the same ideas or beliefs seem to naturally group together to support each other or achieve the common goals that energizes between them. The Universal Law of Fellowship attracts individuals with mutual thoughts or vibrations such as congregations that unite together in a common faith. It also entails groups with ideas that may be harmful to others or fight against the issues that they don't support or agree with or understand.

This law has much power because of the similar vibrations that radiate from each individual, thus making the whole of the group influential or forceful depending on the reason for the gathering. Groups of two or more can bring about or affect others in a very positive and uplifting way or it can be a menacing group which brings to others harm and intimidation.

There are many titled groups that gather with the same purpose for growth, fun, or support of any kind. Such as the Boy Scouts or the Girl Scouts, basketball or baseball teams, or environmental groups that have the desire to protect or save the needs of nature or animals. Fellowshipping at its best is a group that has at its core the goodness of humankind and the protection of God's creations. Groups that support belief in God and His teachings which only raises our own spirits to higher levels of existing.

Jesus blessed the lives of many individuals who gathered around Him for his teachings, His love, His spirit, and His blessings. Those who are divine carry a certain loving attraction that brings many of like souls to their side. Multitudes followed and gathered at Jesus's feet to feel his godly power and his sincere love. Those with like hearts of charity, kindness, and gratitude affect the lives of struggling individuals, thus barring them up and making them stronger. Fellowshipping or accumulating as like individuals can be a great force for good upon the earth. There is strength in numbers.

Parable of Fellowship

There once was a stick that wanted to be a chair, but try as he might, he could not hold up the weight of the seat by himself. "I need support from other sticks who want to be a chair too," he said. So three other such sticks took each corner of the seat, and they all became a chair together.

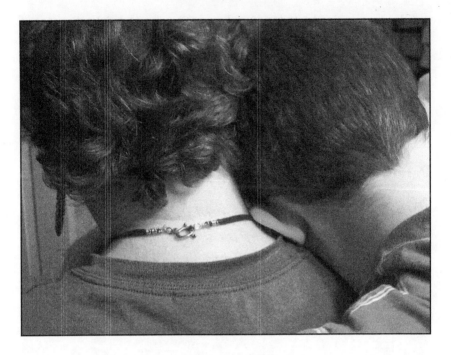

Photo credit: Unhindered by Talent via Visualhunt.com / CC BY-SA

When you forgive, you in no way change the
past—but you sure do change the future.

—Bernard Meltzer, 1916–1998)

14. The Universal Law of Forgiveness.

The Universal Law of Forgiveness is one that brings great
peace and better health to an individual who is holding on
to past mistakes from others as well as from themselves.
Past misdeeds from others, intentionally or not, that were
not corrected and neutralized, holds you back from freedom of peace. Because the one offended holds onto hurts
and "done wrongs" which puts an unseen weight on the
heart and negative feelings in the mind. [42AR]

Word offenses from others come from them and their thinking, their thoughts are not your thoughts and their opinions are not yours. Having the ability to disconnect what others say to you or about you from yourself and having them "own" their own thoughts puts a kind of shield around you. You know the truth, others just have their opinions. They are not in your shoes, so to speak. One can listen to what others have to say in an open and kind way, but then has the ability to take that communication and have it fall away or use it to improve themselves if necessary. Fighting back does more harm to yourself. If a response is necessary, make it a positive one on behalf of yourself and the other person.

Sins or mistakes are always in the past. We either recognize them as soon as they are committed or realize there was an offense as time revealed it. Nonetheless, corrections or repentance needs to replace the burden and right the wrong, thus giving more health to your body because of much less guilt and stress. In order to give strength to your soul, you need to release any negative thoughts or feelings that may have accumulated, and then, by thus doing so, recharges your soul with positive vibrations and uplifting freedom. When we truly repent of past errors in disobedience, God "remembers them no more" (see below #2), but then we still have the memory to help prevent us from committing the same error again. However, we do need to forgive ourselves and move forward with our eye on better performance of choices and faith.

When we tolerate sins or guilt or mistakes, they become as heavy burdens to carry. Burdens that can weigh a person down in countenance, health, and happiness. Removing these oppressive markers in our lives clears or erases them from our choice slate, making it clean again and ready to write a better story for our lives. Not only must we forgive ourselves but also forgive others, thus freeing both of you. Forgiveness is the water that washes away mistrust, hard feelings, hurts, bad choices, or any other negative action. We just need to make the choice to pour the water on and not hold onto dirt because of ego issues.

Blessings or Consequences in the Scriptures for the Universal Law of Forgiveness

1. **Isaiah 1:18 –** <u>Repent</u> **= Sins White As Snow**
   "Come now, and let us reason together, saith the Lord: <u>though your sins be as scarlet,</u> **they shall be as white as snow;** <u>though they be red like crimson,</u> **they shall be as wool."**

2. **Hebrews 8:12 –** <u>Sins</u> **= Remember No More**
   "For I will be merciful to their <u>unrighteousness, and their sins and their iniquities</u> **will I remember no more."**

3. **Matthew 6:12 –** <u>Forgive</u> **= Debtors**
   "<u>And forgive us our debts, as we forgive</u> **our debtors."**

4. **Mosiah 26:29–31 –** <u>Those Who Repent</u> **= Forgive**
   Therefore I say unto you, Go; and whosoever transgresseth against me, him shall ye judge according to the sins which he has committed; **and** <u>if he confess his sins before thee and me, and</u>

<u>repenteth in the sincerity of his heart</u>, **him shall ye forgive, and I will forgive him also.**

Yea, and <u>as often as my people repent</u> **will I forgive them their trespasses against me.**

And ye shall also forgive one another your trespasses; for verily I say unto you, he that forgiveth not his neighbor's trespasses when he says that he repents, the same hath brought himself under condemnation.

5. **Luke 23:34 –** <u>Jesus</u> **= Forgave Soldiers**
   "Then <u>said Jesus,</u> **Father, forgive them; for they know not what they do. And they parted his raiment, and cast lots."**

6. **Ephesians 4:31-32 –** <u>Forgive</u> **= One Another**
   <u>Let all bitterness, and wrath, and anger, and clamour, and evil speaking, be put away from you,</u> **with all malice; And be ye kind one to another, tenderhearted, forgiving one another,** <u>even as God for Christ's sake</u> **hath forgiven you.**

7. **D&C 64:9–10 –** <u>Everyone</u> **= Forgive Each Other**
   Wherefore, <u>I say unto you,</u> **that ye ought to forgive one another; for he that forgiveth not his brother his trespasses standeth condemned before the Lord; for there remaineth in him the greater sin.**

   <u>I, the Lord,</u> **will forgive whom I will forgive,** <u>but of you</u> **it is required to forgive all men.**

8. **D&C 98:40 –** <u>Forgive</u> **= Seventy Times Seven**
    And again, verily I say unto you, if after <u>thine enemy</u> has come upon thee the first time, he repent and come unto thee <u>praying thy for-giveness,</u> thou shalt forgive him, and shalt hold it no more as a testimony against thine enemy. And so on unto the second and third time; and <u>as oft as thine enemy repenteth</u> of the trespass wherewith he has trespassed against thee, thou shalt forgive him, until seventy times seven.

9. **1 Nephi 7:20–21 –** <u>Sorrow Repentance</u> **= Forgiveness**
    And it came to pass that <u>they were sorrowful,</u> because of their wickedness, insomuch that <u>they did bow down before me, and did plead with me</u> that I would forgive them of the thing that they had done against me. And it came to pass that I did frankly forgive them all that they had done, and I did exhort them that they would pray unto the Lord their God for forgiveness . . .

10. **D&C 58:43 –** <u>Sins</u> **= Confess and Forsake Them**
    "By this ye may know <u>if a man repenteth of his sins</u>- behold, he will confess them and forsake them."

Summary

The Universal Law of Forgiveness is a valuable action that frees a person's soul from spirit prison. For those who continuously hold on to offenses, mistakes, hurts, and guilt, carry an extremely heavy burden that tears down the spirit and the body. Forgiveness is the ultimate release of weights that gives a person freedom and an opportunity to start again or to let go and give both themselves and others a new level of vibration of living—a higher frequency of love.

Jesus taught that forgiveness was required of everyone, seventy times seven, if they repent (see #8 above), if they try to make it right, if they apologize. If the offending person does their best to right the wrong, then the other person carries the burden if they do not accept the act of forgiveness. In D&C 18:13, Jesus said, "And how great is his joy in the soul that repenteth!" It makes perfect sense or it stands to reason that when one lets go of a burden of guilt, freedom and great relief will follow. So it would be ridiculous (in my mind) not to want to make this state of being a reality, at least for the good of your own health.

Sometimes we don't actually realize that we have a "parasite" within our subconscious that has been feeding on a past action that grows guilt or vengeance or resentment within us. This "bug" may someday grow to the extent that it affects our progression because of its influence to hold us back. We need to recognize this condition in our minds, forgive the action or the offender, and let loose of the feeling before it drags us down or erupts or eats away at our souls. Forgiveness is a true freedom. It is like setting down a fifty-pound backpack that you have been carrying around for years—what a relief! And your spirit soars to greater heights of love, peace, and joy!

Using this most important Universal Law of Forgiveness—forgive yourself, forgive others. We all make mistakes. It just happens, so we all need to be kind to ourselves and those around us. With love and understanding, forgive, forget, and be free.

Parable of Forgiveness

Behold, a leather bag with carrying straps was stuffed with heavy past human mistakes and judgments. This annoying bag weighed down the shoulders of the person lugging it around day after day. What was interesting was instead of pulling each mistake out of the bag and discarding it, the person opened the bag only to add even more problems into it—which made it even more uncomfortable to support. The solution to the situation was easy—but a little hard. It was just to slip open the flap and make restitution for every wrong or forgive the issue. Then the bag would be removed. The person could stand up tall and see the sun shining again in their soul. How silly it is to keep the bag.

Photo credit: Kiwi Tom via Visual hunt / CC BY

Behold, here is wisdom, and let
every man choose for himself.

—D&C 37:4

15. The Universal Law of Free Will or Law of Choice.

Certainly, if there is one Universal Law that has always been
(of course there are many) affecting people the most in form-
ing their quality of existence, it's this one. Everything we do
requires a choice of some kind or another, and the beauty
of it all is that *we* can make whatever choice we want. We
are the captain of our minds and thoughts no matter our
circumstance or surroundings. How we choose to think,
how we choose to act, how we choose to decide between

this or that or what we choose to believe or support. This Law, that originated from God to give His children agency to make choices for themselves which way their lives would go, to obey any law or not, cut the strings of control, and placed the responsibility onto ourselves to form the life we live (see scriptures below). [43AR]

If our present situation in life doesn't quite fit into what we expected or desired, then we have the choice to change it, to make it better, to accomplish our dreams as desired and visualized to be. Or it could just be a change of attitude or of gratitude. Whichever the case, freedom of choice is a gift of mind born within all people. The use of our imagination and our creativity to accomplish things, to acquire things, to build abilities and knowledge, is just a matter of deciding to do so, make plans of how to, and then moving toward that goal.

The Law of Choice {44} is also a law that gives us the ability to act or react to things that come at us. We can either choose to hastily react to an uncomfortable communication—which usually does no good for anyone—or to listen, think, and then decide to respond with full faculties in place or to disconnect and let it go. We can agree to build a positive mind with uplifting thoughts, thus accumulating a higher level of existence, or to select a negative attitude and gather grief, pain, and few accomplishments.

Though it may be easy to blame others and circumstances to account for our present reality, it still boils down to ourselves and our choices of how we choose to live or choose to act. We have the choice to continually move forward in growth and love or backward the other direction which leads to sadness and despair. The wonderful thing is that when you choose happiness with a heart full of sharing, you will reap the same thing, thus everyone wins. Society is much better off with citizens that decide to dwell on a higher level of peace, love, and joy. Choosing to live all the natural and spiritual laws will always bring blessings and enlightenment which will give us great joy and fulfillment in attaining our life's purpose.

However, the Law of Free Will or Choice is also our constant, refining teacher. We learn by our choices what to do different or better next time. There is no failure in life, only learning experiences or challenges that expand our hearts and abilities. We only move backward if we stop or give up, and even then, we still are gaining wisdom of what not to do or how it feels like to live in a dark or difficult place. By coming out of these realms of lower existence, a person can help others from doing so because of the experience they had from dwelling there.

So from moment to moment, we have the freedom born within us to make decisions for ourselves about how our lives are going, or how our lives will develop tomorrow or in the future. Do we select this or that? Will this choice be good for me or not? Will I express love and gratitude or notice everything with a negative approach? "Choose you this day whom you will serve" (#2 below). Which road will you take your life down or do you need to turn around and travel up a different road that is meant more for you? Also, realizing that whatever the final decision is, you will handle the consequences or results of your decision with grace or indifference, but what materializes from choices is what automatically comes—which also entails the Universal Law of Cause and Effect. It's up to you, you decide!

Blessings or Consequences in the Scriptures for the Universal Law of Free Will or Law of Choice

1. **Moses 3:17**– Choose To Eat = **Know Good and Evil**

    But of the tree of the knowledge of good and evil, thou shalt not eat of it, **nevertheless,** thou mayest choose for thyself, **for it is given unto thee; but, remember that I forbid it, for in the day** thou eatest **thereof thou shalt surely die.**

2. **Joshua 24:15** – Choose = **To Serve The Lord**

    And if it seem evil unto you to serve the Lord, choose you this day **whom ye will serve; whether the gods which your fathers served that were on the other side of the flood, or the gods of the Amorites, in whose land ye swell;** but as for me and my house, **we will serve the Lord.**

3. **2 Nephi 10:23** – God Gave Man = **Freedom To Act For Himself**

    "Therefore, cheer up your hearts, and remember that ye are free to act for yourselves— **to choose the way of everlasting death or the way of eternal life."**

4. **Alma 12:31** – Choose = **Good or Evil**

    Wherefore, he gave commandments unto men, they having first transgressed the first commandments as to things which were temporal, and becoming as God, knowing good from evil, placing themselves in a state to act,

or being placed in a state to act according to their wills and pleasures, whether to do evil or to do good—

5. **Helaman 14:30–31** – Act for Yourself = **Choose Good or Evil**

    And now remember, remember, my brethren, that whosoever perisheth, perisheth unto himself; and whosoever doeth iniquity, doeth it unto himself; for behold, ye are free; ye are permitted to act for yourselves; **for behold, God hath given unto you a** knowledge and he hath made you free. **He hath given unto you** that ye **might know good from evil, and he hath given unto you that** ye might choose **life or death; and** ye **can do good and be restored unto that which is good, or have that which is good restored unto you;** or ye can **do evil, and have that which is evil restored unto you.**

6. **D&C 29:36** – One Third of Heaven = **Chose Another Way**

    "For he rebelled against me, saying, Give me thine honor, which is my power; and also a third part of the hosts of heaven **turned he away from me because of their agency;"**

7. **D&C 37:4** – Every Man = **Freedom to Choose**

    "Behold, here is wisdom, and let every man **choose for himself until I come. Even so. Amen."**

8. **D&C 98:8** – <u>The Law</u> = **Makes You Free**

   "I, the <u>Lord God</u>, **make you free, therefore ye are free indeed; and** <u>the law</u> **also maketh you free.**"

9. **Mosiah 2:21** – <u>God</u> = **Freedom to Live and Move**

   <u>Serve him who has created you from the beginning,</u> **and is preserving you from day to day, by lending you breath, that ye may live and move and do according to your own will, and even supporting you from one moment to another . . .**

10. **2 Nephi 2:27** – <u>Man Are Free</u> = **To Choose Liberty or Captivity**

    Wherefore, <u>men are free</u> **according to the flesh; and all things are given them which are expedient unto man. And** <u>they are free</u> **to choose liberty and eternal life, through the great Mediator of all men, or to choose captivity and death, according to the captivity and power of the devil; for he seeketh that all men might be miserable like unto himself.**

Summary

The Universal Law of Free Will or the Law of Choice gives everyone the freedom and the responsibility to make choices and accept the outcome of those selected choices.

Our whole life centers around making decisions about one thing or another every moment of the day and each choice forms the result of our lives. Thus, being aware of how we choose from one source to another could make a big difference on the path our life takes.

The actions of the world come from agency of choice, be it for good or for ill. God gave us all the opportunity to make whatever choice we decide to perform. He also gave us the ability to handle the consequence of our choice, be it happily or miserably—it is all our own making. God also gives us rich blessing for choosing to obey his command-ments, his laws. Choosing the righteous path always brings the highest blessings. It is similar to parents rewarding their own children for making correct choices, praising them for their good thoughts and actions.

Our thoughts are our own, we are responsible for what we do and say. We are responsible for peace or disruption, depending on the actions we choose to perform. Our choices also affect those around us. They either spread positive bet-terment or unkindness. There are always choices to make throughout our every day that form our future and either build our character with integrity or pull it down. Choosing to love ourselves and those around us brings peace, encour-agement, health, and wealth. Be aware of what your choices are and make an effort to choose the best possible selection for yourself, your future, and the benefit of mankind.

Parable of Free Will/Choice

Once there was an ant that was searching for small round things to eat for food. While scurrying around under a berry bush, the bush would wave its small branches above the ant's busy body to choose its sweet fruit for food, but the little ant with its feelers to the ground, kept selecting hard gray pebbles instead. Once the ant gathered enough to put into its food bowl, it tried to eat the hard nuggets but discovered it had chosen round objects of the wrong kind. Rolling out the pebbles, it quickly slipped back under the berry bush to accept the tiny red berries that the bush offered and found them very nourishing and sweet indeed.

Photo credit: Ian Sane via Visual Hunt / CC BY

For it is in giving that we receive.

—Francis of Assisi, 1181–1226

16. The Universal Law of Giving and Receiving.

The Universal Law of Giving and Receiving originates from the heart of the giver and responses in kind—touching the heart of the receiver. It is one that has the base of love at its core. To give is to get out of oneself for the benefit of another. Seeing another in need or just passing on a smile or an appreciation brings joyous results for both sides.

The Lord placed a high value on this law by instructing all to help those in need and by doing so, it would be as if you gave to the Savior himself. [45AR]

Energy flows from one person to another, from one plant to another, and around all things and through all things. Giving and receiving is like a constant, continuous flow of love energy that rises every individual it touches. It is similar to the ebb and flow of the ocean—in and out, among and through spirits for the betterment of the mind and soul of man. If one side gets stopped or "scrooged" (held back and not shared), the flow of love energy is halted and becomes stagnant, there is no giving or receiving.

Everyone recognizes the benefit of this law. Everyone enjoys a smile, a hug, or a gift. It is a way to express gratitude, appreciation, and caring. Not only is it important to give something, but it is also as important to take the gesture graciously without refusing the gift. By not accepting a gift or an offering of help or anything of such service is like telling the person giving that you do not appreciate their gift or their time, thus they are not blessed, and neither are you. If one does not need anything or help, at least accepting the kindness of the giver's heart with full gratitude and praise keeps all feelings in a positive, flowing continuum.

The idea is the same with wealth and money. If you give more, you receive more. Keeping currency flowing keeps the abundance going out and coming back to use, grow, and keep circulating it for everyone. There is no lack. Abundance is unlimited and is attracted to you by your positive thinking, generosity, and effort to produce. If you want more of anything, then give that same thing away. If you want love, then give love. If you want more friends, then be a good friend—but the giving is first before the receiving. Don't sit around waiting for things to happen to you, you must, and for most, first give. Think of others before your own concerns, and what you give away will come back to you.

One of God's Laws is the paying of tithes and offerings—a giving and receiving commandment (see #1 below). By following this instruction, one can help the church by building His kingdom with the construction of church buildings and temples and thus, by doing so, the giver receives great blessings from the Lord. The Law of Giving also forms an individual's character to be more generous and less selfish. It is also a way to sacrifice one's belongings or wealth to help another who is low or who needs assistance in attaining the things they need.

Receiving also gives the recipient the opportunity to turn around and become the giver, thus the action forms an eternal round, energy to energy—keeping the flow of unselfishness and gratitude continuously surging in and through all things carrying high levels of peace, love, and joy, thus creating a more caring and loving world. Jesus being the prime example of how to manifest the use of giving to high levels of sacrifice and love. We can follow His example in our everyday by sharing, servicing, understanding, giving gifts, and love to those who mean the most to us and then spreading that movement to our neighbor. What a wonderful world it would be if that were so.

Blessings or Consequences in the Scriptures for the Universal Law of Giving and Receiving

1. **Malachi 3:10** – <u>Give Tithing</u> = **Receive Blessings**
   <u>Bring ye all the tithes</u> **into the storehouse, that there may be meat in mine house, and prove me now herewith, saith the Lord of hosts, if I will not open you the windows of heaven, and pour**

you out a blessing, that there shall not be room enough to receive it.

2. **Matthew 10:8** – <u>Freely Receive</u> = **Freely Give**
   "**Heal the sick, cleanse the lepers, raise the dead, cast out devils;** <u>freely ye have received,</u> **freely give.**"

3. **Matthew 5:42** – <u>Give</u> = **Turn Not Away**
   "<u>Give to him that asketh thee,</u> **and** <u>from him that would borrow</u> **of thee turn not thou away.**"

4. **Matthew 25:40** – <u>Done To The Least</u> = **Done to God**
   "**And the King shall answer and say unto them, Verily I say unto you, Inasmuch as ye have** <u>done it unto one of the least of these my brethren,</u> **ye have done it unto me.**"

5. **Acts 20:35** – <u>More Blessed to Give</u> = **Than Receive**
   "**To remember the words of the Lord Jesus, how he said, It is** <u>more blessed to give</u> **than to receive.**"

6. **Matthew 19:29** – <u>Those Who Gave</u> = **Receive Hundredfold**
   "**And everyone that** <u>hath forsaken</u> **houses, or brethren, or sister, or father, or mother, or wife, or children, or lands, for my name's sake, shall receive an hundredfold, and shall inherit everlasting life.**"

7. **Deuteronomy 16:17 –** <u>Give</u> **= As Able**
    "Every man shall <u>give</u> as he is able, according to the blessing of the Lord thy God which he hath given thee."

8. **2 Corinthians 9:7 –** <u>Give</u> **= Cheerfully**
    "Every man according as he purposeth in his heart, <u>so let him give; not grudgingly, or of necessity:</u> for God loveth a cheerful giver."

9. **D&C 42:33 –** <u>Give</u> **= To Those in Need**
    "It shall be kept to <u>administer</u> to those who have not, from time to time, that every man who has need <u>may be amply supplied</u> and receive according to his wants."

10. **Proverbs 21:26 –** <u>Righteous Giver</u> **= Spareth Not**
    "He coveteth greedily all the day long: but <u>the righteous giveth</u> and spareth not."

Summary

The Law of Giving and Receiving requires one to take some of their spirit out of themselves and actually reach out and give away something meaningful that came from their heart. In giving, we take a piece of ourselves and share it with someone else. In so doing, the receiver graciously accepts the offering and adds it to their accumulation of love in their heart, ready to give that away again, thus the cycle goes around and around, giving strength to each other. Rising each other up to a higher level of sacrifice, of receiving, of positive living.

The first step in receiving is in the giving. The more we give, the more we will receive. This is a Universal Law that is true to its name. However, one must be in the right frame of mind having a gracious attitude to give anything appropriately. Feeling like you have to give or you have to serve or you have to share does not carry a high vibration of love, it moves forward a lower feeling of regret or selfishness—which serves no one in a positive way and halts blessings and stifles the giving/receiving flow. Jesus counseled us in the scriptures to give cheerfully and not grudgingly.

Nature gives and receives through its cycles of life as well. The nutrient earth gives plants or seeds its rich soil to generate in, and through time, the plant returns its nutrients and minerals back into the soil once its life is complete, to produce life once again. The falling of rain to the earth and then evaporates up again gives supply for future waterings. Everything gives, and everything receives. Life's rhythms of give and take, replenishing and using, circulating out and returning back.

Pleasure is generated from giving and receiving. It touches the heart strings and brings joy to both sides. It's like throwing out handfuls of happiness seeds wherever you go and having them blossom to delicate flowers to be picked by everyone. And then receiving a beautiful bouquet from the seeds you sowed. It keeps the wonderful moments of being continuous and ongoing, bringing brightness to everyone concerned, because of the action of the heart.

Parable of Giving and Receiving

There stood a certain man upon a high ridge that could see far and wide. Holding in his hand was a specially crafted wooden boomerang that, with the flick of his wrist, sent it sailing into the air. Round and round it went until it found its way back to the man, and he caught it easily. No matter where he stood or where he went, when he let it spin through the air, it always found its way back home to him—and so it is with giving and receiving.

Photo credit: ^@^ina (Irina Patrascu Gheorghita)
via VisualHunt.com / CC BY

Cultivate the habit of being grateful for
every good thing that comes to you, and give
thanks continuously. And because all things
have contributed to your advancement, you
should include all things in your gratitude.

—Ralph Waldo Emerson

17. The Universal Law of Gratitude.

Following the Law of Giving and Receiving, we have the
natural consequence in feeling the art of gratitude. Being
grateful for what we have been blessed with or have been
given shows the giver or the maker how pleased we are with
what we have received.

No matter how large or minuscule our belongings may be, an "attitude of gratitude" {46} will only bring the possibility of more. [47AR] "Count your many blessings" are the words to a familiar hymn which are very worthy of our attention and expression. {48} Once a person "opens their eyes" to everything they have and everything that is around them that is good and worthy, one realizes just how abundant their lives are. Blessings are not just in physical belongings, but it emanates through all of nature that so generously abounds for our joy and benefit. To appreciate the wonders of ballooning clouds touched by the pink of sunset or the crystal clear waters of a mountain stream surrounded by whispering trees and sweet grasses. The magnificence of God's creation, it is truly amazing, and one would be extremely ungrateful if they did not appreciate it and give eternal thanks to God for His creative abilities and love.

"Thank you," as in the previous law chapter of Giving and Receiving, are two words that should come forth easily and often. The more we express appreciation, the more we give results in receiving more. However, there may be some situations or challenges that seem to only bring us to a negative level and that is where we must force a notice of what is good or what to be grateful for in those times of trial. Hard situations, if dealt with well, bring us growth, patience, and appreciation. Did not Christ suffer the most and did the result of His suffering save us all and gave Him the honor of completing His assigned mission—which is to love and save us all?

As you can imagine and have already experienced for yourself, that when another person is appreciative of what you have given them, your spirit is touched, and you have a growing desire to give that person more—as in the case of a parent to a grateful child. God is exactly like that, and He is very uncomfortable when his children do not show or express a grateful heart for even the smallest of blessings. {49} God is here to help us, to bless us throughout our lives in every challenge that comes our way. Be grateful for the knowledge of that eternal truth.

Thank-you cards are easily purchased, or even better, take a moment and construct one of your own make and freely deliver them out in abundance—your heart will have fun and be uplifted upward to a higher vibration of love, and those receiving will develop the same. Thus, at this time, I feel it appropriate to tell everyone who has taken time to read this book of Laws and Blessings, *thank you*, I truly appreciate it and hope in a multitude of ways that this book is very beneficial and enlightening to you for the betterment of your life! It has been very uplifting in mine.

Blessings or Consequences in the Scriptures for the Universal Law of Gratitude

1. **Luke 17:15–18** – <u>Person Healed </u>= **Gave Thanks**
    And one of them, when he saw that he <u>was healed, turned back,</u> **and with a loud voice glorified God. And fell** <u>down on his face at his feet, giving him</u> **thanks: and he was a Samaritan. And Jesus answering said, Were there not ten cleansed? But where are the nine?**

2.   **Mosiah 2:19** – <u>Give Thanks</u> = **To Heavenly King**
     "And behold also, if I, whom ye call your king, who has spent his days inn your service, and yet has been in the service of **God,** <u>do merit any thanks from you,</u> **O how** <u>you ought to thank</u> your heavenly King!"

3.   **D&C 46:32** – <u>Give Thanks</u> = **For Your Blessings**
     "And ye must <u>give thanks unto God</u> in the Spirit for whatsoever blessing ye are blessed with."

4.   **D&C 78:19** – <u>Give Thanks</u> = **Receive Hundredfold**
     "And he who <u>receiveth all things with thankfulness</u> shall be made glorious; and the things of this earth shall be added unto him, even as hundred fold, yea, more."

5.   **D&C 136:28** – <u>Praise</u> = **With Singing and Dancing**
     "If thou art merry, <u>praise the Lord</u> with singing, with music, with dancing, and with a prayer of praise and thanksgiving."

6.   **Alma 34:38** – <u>Be Thankful</u> = **For God's Mercies**
     That ye humble yourselves even to the dust, and worship God, in whatsoever place ye may be in, in spirit and in truth; and <u>that ye live in thanksgiving daily,</u> **for the many mercies and blessings which he doth bestow upon you.**

7. **D&C 59:21** – <u>God</u> = **Enjoys Obedience**

"<u>And in nothing doth man offend God, </u>**or against none is his wrath kindles, save those who confess not his hand in all things, and obey not his commandments.**"

8. **Revelation 7:12** – <u>Thanksgiving </u>= **To God Forever**

"**Saying, Amen:** <u>Blessing, and glory, and wisdom, and thanksgiving, and honour, and power, and might</u>, **be unto our God for ever and ever. Amen.**"

9. **Philippians 4:6** – <u>Requests To God</u> = **With Thanksgiving**

"**Be careful for nothing; but in every thing by prayer and supplication with thanksgiving** <u>let your requests be made known unto God.</u>"

10. **D&C 62:7** – <u>Be Thankful</u> = **To God for All Things**

"**I, the Lord, am willing, if any among you desire to ride upon horses, or upon mules, or in chariots, he shall receive this blessing, if** <u>he receive it from the hand of the lord, with a thankful heart</u> **in all things.**"

Summary

Each Universal Law or Laws of God, when followed according to the law's requirements, produces blessings immediately or in time. Being grateful for positive compensations of obedience, which multiples when appreciation is noticed and acknowledged. Gratitude is the icing on the cake of giving and receiving. Without appreciation, the "cake" doesn't quite taste as good on the tongue, something is missing. Giving "thanks" for gifts or smiles or anything else received spreads the delights of the spirit to all involved, and the urge or desire to do more swells inside our hearts—basically because it is fun, and it just seems right to reply appropriately.

As in the form of humble, expressed prayer, giving thanks is the first tender words that begin a prayer. {50} We shouldn't ask for anything without first appreciating all that God has blessed us with. Sometimes just a prayer focused entirely on gratitude without supplication of wants is the best prayer of all.

When one realizes how much abundance there is in their life and the magnitude of blessings in the form of nature is outstanding and must be appreciated with words of thanksgiving, often and continually in the heart. It doesn't matter if a person has a bounty of possessions or a scant supply, there is so much outside of them to be grateful for, let alone the talents, spirit, and intelligence potential that is born within their soul.

And again, I express my appreciation for having the opportunity to study eternal laws and share them in book form for anyone who is interested in knowing which blessings are produced from obedience to which laws. To be able to bless more of their life and connect more with God who gives everyone the ability and capacity to reach their full potential of greatness. I pass on a thank-you thought to everyone out there, and especially, to my Father in Heaven.

Parable of Gratitude

In the days of wagons and metal milk cans, there was a delivery man who delivered a gallon of milk each day to two households. One of the homes was so gracious and thankful for their milk that the delivery man always received a flower or a pie (depending on if it was bake day or not). He loved delivering milk those days to that family—it made him very happy.

The other house was not usually even aware that the delivery man had even put the milk on their porch, let alone received anything. Not even a nod or a "that's nice." It wasn't fun delivering to them, but he quickly did it anyway. Not even at Christmas was there a card for him. The delivery man gave extra milk to the grateful family at Christmas. More blessings always come with a grateful heart.

Photo via Visual hunt

Let food be thy medicine and
medicine by thy food.

—Hippocrates

18. The Universal Law of Health.

Certain elements are required to sustain proper developing
health of body as well as in the natural world. To have everything needed to germinate, grow, and mature is a must in
promoting healthy plant life as well as animal life. Things
cannot evolve into their predetermined state on substance
that does not feed health or wholeness. Living things will
either thrive or die depending on the quality of nourish-
ment they attain. Anything will dwindle away and die
unless it accumulates or takes in what it has been designed

to eat to survive and thrive. Even developing stars need certain elements and materials to sustain their formation.

All living beings require other living and well things to live and reach their maximum health ability. Certain animals either feed off of green, nutrient-rich grasses or leaves while other mammals gather meals from other animals that are or were alive and living. Plants soak up energy from the sun and nutrients from the earth mixed with necessary water, then animals and mankind eat these rich plants engulfing life cells with stamina and health. God designed the most nutrient foods available for man and beast. Thus, the purest, freshest, most desirable food for health comes from Gods' creations, not man's.

Not only is food necessary for healthy living, but also in the recipe is the proper amount of rest, fresh air, pure water, positive thinking, and low stress. Pollution, dirty water, or a high-stress, busy existence does not promote a healthy body or mind. The Law of Health spans multiple ingredients to sustain as much health as possible. Sicknesses may come and go to a much lower degree given the amount of proper attention to the correct nutrition and environment as much as possible, and for a fair amount of lifetime. Many diseases are preventable by eating the right foods that God created for our health and wellbeing. [51AR]

There seems to be a fair amount of disagreement of exactly what to partake of, so I will only present the laws as they are written, and you can decide for yourself. There are scads of books and information available on the topic, but in my opinion, our true maker above knows what is best for our welfare and care—which is presented in the Word of Wisdom, {52} which is a scriptural revelation from God about what he prefers we eat for our best health. And also what has been recorded in the scriptures for our learning. Nonetheless, I will mention eight areas that are laws for good health and wellness of body and mind. First, nutrition—natural, fresh food. Second, exercise—working, movement, play. Third, water—pure, clean drinkable water. Fourth, sunlight—enough sun to replenish vitamins and spirit. Fifth, temperance—to avoid harmful substances. Sixth, air—clean, nonpolluted breathing. Seventh, rest— seven to nine hours is desirable for rejuvenation. Eighth, trust—in God to bless you for your health efforts and life. When we are the master of our physical condition, we are more in master of our lives in confidence and achievements. President Thomas S. Monson taught that "God gave man life and with it the power to think and reason and decide and love. With such power given to you and to me, mastery of self becomes a necessity if we are to have the abundant life." {53} Thus, having habits of health brings forth more ability to enjoy the wonders of living.

Nature requires similar life giving sources for proper growth, good nutrient soil, decent water, fresh air, sunshine and sufficient time for generation and growth. Everything is energy and everything has comparable needs to produce life and fulfill it's purpose and measurement of what it was created to do. Even the heavens require sources that they are composed of to form and complete their function. Pretty much, if you do not have good health or sufficient mental abilities, you are very limited on the choices of fulfillment that you have in your life.

Blessings or Consequences in the Scriptures for the Universal Law of Health

1. Daniel 1:12–15 – <u>Eat Pulse not Meat of King</u> = Healthy

    Prove thy servants, I beseech thee, ten days; and let them <u>give us pulse to eat, and water to drink.</u>

    Then let our countenances be looked upon before thee, and the countenance of the children that eat of the portion of the king's meat; and as thou seest, deal with thy servants. So he consented to them in this matter, and proved them ten days. And at the end of ten days their countenances appeared fairer and fatter in flesh than all the children which did eat the portion of the king's meat.

2. D&C 42:43 – <u>Nourish</u> = With Herbs

    "And whosoever among you are sick, and have not faith to be healed, but believe, shall be <u>nourished with all tenderness,</u> with herbs and mild food, and that not by the hand of an enemy."

3. D&C 59:17–19 – <u>Good Things of the Earth</u> = For Food

    Yea, <u>and the herb, and the good things which come of the earth,</u> whether for food or for raiment, or for houses, or for barns, or for orchards, or for gardens, or for vineyards; Yea, <u>all things which come of the earth, in the season thereof,</u> are made for the benefit and the use of man, both to please the eye and to gladden the heart; Yea, for food and for raiment, for taste and for smell, to strengthen the body and to enliven the soul.

4. **Alma 46:40** – Herbs and Plants = **Cure Disease**
    But not so much so with fevers, because of the excellent qualities of the many plants and roots which God had prepared to remove the cause of diseases, to which men were subject by the nature of the climate—

5. **Ezekiel 47:12** – Plants = **For Meat and Medicine**
    "It shall bring forth new fruit according to his months, because their waters they issued out of the sanctuary: and the fruit thereof shall be for meat, and the leaf thereof for medicine.'

6. **D&C 89:7–9** – Drinks & Tobacco = **Not Good for Man**
    And, again, strong drinks are not for the belly, but for the washing of your bodies. And again, tobacco is not for the body, neither for the belly, and is not good for man, but is an herb for bruises and all sick cattle, to be used with judgment and skill. And again, hot drinks are not for the body or belly,

7. **D&C 89:10–11** – Herbs and Fruits = **Good to Eat**
    And again, verily I say unto you, all wholesome herbs God hath ordained for the constitution, nature, and use of ma — Every herb in

the season thereof, and every fruit in the season thereof; **all these to be used with prudence and thanksgiving.**

8. **Genesis 2:8–9 –** Fruit **= Good for Food**
    And the Lord God planted a garden eastward in Eden; and there he put the man whom he had formed. And out of the ground made the Lord God to grow every tree **that is pleasant to the sight, and good for food: . . .**

9. **D&C 89:12–13 –** Meat **= To Eat Sparingly**
    Yea, flesh also of beasts and of the fowls **of the air, I, the lord, have ordained for the use of man with thanksgiving; nevertheless they are to be used sparingly; And it is pleasing unto me that they should not be used, only in times of winter, or of cold, or famine.**

10. **D&C 89:14, 16 –** Grains **= Good for Food**
    All grain **is ordained for the use of man and of beasts, to be the staff of life, not only for man but for the beasts of the field, and the fowls of heaven, and all wild animals that run or creep on the earth,**
    All grain **is good for the food of man; as also the fruit of the vine;** that which yieldeth fruit, whether in the ground or above the ground—

Summary

All living creatures and vegetation need specific and consistent sources of nutrients, water, and sunshine to reach their maximum strength and longevity. To achieve the pinnacle of wellness desired, the health sources need to be at their purest form. Water needs to be clear and clean, not murky and polluted. Food sources need to be naturally grown, not covered with chemicals or manipulated at their seedling to grow into something not God designed.

Since God created mankind, it stands to reason that God knows how best to care for the human body. Scripture verses relay the directed health code from God to his children (see #55) that were created in His own image. {54} I think we all know instinctively which foods constitute the building of a strong physique and disease-free organs. It is unanimous that fresh fruits and vegetables play a big part in how healthy cells can be, thus consuming a lot of factory processed, unnatural food with high amounts of sugar and artificial fillers produce a body that is headed in the direction of ill health and disease.

Along with life giving life to all creation, other elements that generate wellness include light, as in sunshine, a sufficient amount of healing sleep, movement in work or exercise, a positive and grateful attitude saturated with love for self and others. Existing in a high level of positive vibrations and frequency sustains peace, love, and joy, which bears the fruits of highest health and living. {55} The opposite consisting of dwelling in mind and body degradation and disease—as the Law of Polarity (Law #25) describes and teaches. Health progression or the opposite end to misery.

It is interesting that everything exists in the state of health progression life cycle, or weakness and incomplete achievement of potential. Even the stars in the universe requires sufficient gases and materials to complete its designed function to form into a complete star; otherwise, they would not quite complete their mission, just to sputter in the attempt or fade away into oblivion. Health means progression and completion of potential. It means enjoyment and fulfillment in everyday achievement. It means the ability to function in a productive manner. By following and obeying the Universal Health Law and God's Health Law, one will accomplish and reside in the best possible health and wellness as one can achieve.

Parable of Health

This is the tale of two carrots seeds. Both were sunk into the warm, rich earth with positive possibility for strong growth. The one received plenty of warm sun and fresh water with nutrients from other plants to give it all it needed to produce its best orange root. The other seed received sun as well, but was sprayed with chemicals mixed with pesticides to kill the so-called bad bugs that were out in nature too. Its orange root soaked up a lot of the poisonous solution, and even though it looked healthy from the outside, inside it was sick. They were both plucked to sell at the market. Which are you eating?

Photo credit: Me now0 via Visual Hunt / CC BY-ND

I believe that God gives you hopes
and dreams in a size that's too large, so
you have something to grow into.

—Lynn A. Robinson

19. The Universal Law of Increase.

This law follows along a constant path. We get more of what we give our most attention to. It stands to reason that what we pay most attention to, we will receive more of. For example, the more I figure out how to manage money and earn or grow more money, the more currency will come into my life. My wealth will increase. If I focus on how my abundance of time that I have (if I believe that or not) or show gratitude for my time, then my time will seem to increase. The same applies to nature. The Universal Law of Increase is built into the cycles of plants and animals. Flowers grow, mature, and spread their increase of seeds everywhere along the wind to attach to the earth, grow, and increase again. The families of animals have a natural instinct to mate, give birth, and increase generations and species after them—the living line continues. Humans continue their lines of family as well with the attraction we have for male and female to produce offspring. We have a natural urge to continue our lines of families and ourselves. [56AR]

If we focus on developing muscle or a stronger, leaner physique, then that result will manifest in an increase in muscle mass. If we have a desire for a more accomplished talent of one kind or another, then the more we practice and focus on learning and achieving, the more increase of ability will develop. The same is true for building up stronger faith or increasing a testimony. The more we put our attention on the subject, the more our abilities will increase in eternal matters or in a firmer spirit about godly things.

Seek more knowledge? Study more, read more in the choice of learning, then your knowledge will increase. Also, the more we obey the Laws of God, the more blessings and abilities will come our way. President Brigham Young enlightened us with positive counsel. He said, "Our religion is worth everything to us and for it we should be willing to employ our time, our talent, our means, our energies, our lives." And, "If we do right, there will be an eternal increase among this people in talent, strength and intellect, and earthly wealth, from this time, henceforth, and forever." {57}

However, this law can be used backward to our detriment. One needs to be aware and careful, for the law also increases what we do not want—if that is our focus. Similar to the Law of Attraction (see Chapter 4), we attract or increase into our lives what our thoughts are most about. If we focus on lack and small amounts of wealth, then we will increase our shortage. But if we appreciate what we do have, small or large, and do our best action to produce more or better ourselves, increase will naturally follow. Wallowing in self-pity or lack of opportunity or perceived shortage of blessings will only increase that situation. Gratitude is the first step to produce increase or attract more positive situations into our lives.

God desires for us, His children, to have abundance, to increase and receive happiness and blessings throughout our lives here on earth. But to increase in anything, we must be aware of the laws and obey the natural laws which will produce abundance into our lives because of our efforts and awareness of positive living. Increase is beneficial for a life full of opportunities to enrich our potential and to help others do the same. Just like the increase we receive from harvesting our bounteous gardens, we need to share our increase to help others who would gratefully appreciate in our giving. That is the whole point of increase—to supply for our own needs and to spread the excess around to others, be it in the form of sharing nutrition or talents for enjoyment or multiplying a new generation. It is for the betterment of mankind.

Blessings or Consequences in the Scriptures for the Universal Law of Increase

1. **Matthew 25:20** – <u>Talents Development</u> = **More**
    "And so he that had received five talents came and brought other five talents, saying, Lord, thou deliveredst unto me five talents: behold, <u>I have gained beside them</u> **five talents more."**

2. **Deuteronomy 16:15** – <u>God Bless</u> = **In Increase**
    "Because the <u>Lord thy God shall bless thee</u> **in all thine increase, and in all the works of thine hands, therefore thou shalt surely rejoice."**

3. **Ezekiel 34:27** – <u>Fruit</u> = **Earth Yield Increase**
    "And the tree of the field shall <u>yield her fruit,</u> **and the earth shall yield her increase, and they shall be safe in their land, and shall know that I am the Lord, . . ."**

4. **Proverbs 9:9** – <u>Teach</u> = **Increase in Learning**
    "<u>Give instruction</u> **to a wise man, and he will be yet wiser;** <u>teach</u> **a just man, and he will increase in learning."**

5.**Alma 32:28–29** – <u>Faith as a Seed</u> = **Grow to Increase**

Now, we will <u>compare the word unto a seed.</u> Now, if ye give place, that a <u>seed may be planted in your heart,</u> <u>behold, if it be a true seed, or a good seed, if ye do not cast it out by your unbelief,</u> that ye will resist the Spirit of the Lord, behold, **it will begin to swell** within your breasts; and when you feel these swelling motions, ye will begin to say within yourselves—It must needs be that this is a good seed, or that the word is good, for **it beginneth to enlarge my soul; yea, it beginneth to enlighten my understanding**, yea, it beginneth to be delicious to me. Now behold, would not this **increase** your faith? I say unto you, Yea; nevertheless it hath not grown up to a perfect knowledge.

6. **D&C 88:118** – Teach and Study = **Increase in Knowledge**
   "And as all have not faith, seek ye diligently and teach one another **words of wisdom; yea,** seek ye out of the best books **words of wisdom; seek learning,** even by study and also by faith.**"**

7. **Luke 2:52** – Jesus = **Increase in Wisdom, Statue and Favor**
   "And Jesus **increased in wisdom and stature, and in favour with God and man.'**

8. **1 Thessalonians 3:12** – Increase = **In Love**
   "And the Lord make you to increase and abound **in love one toward another, and toward all men, even as we do toward you:"**

9. **Genesis 1:28** – Adam and Eve = **Multiply and Replenish the Earth**
   "And God blessed them, and God said unto them, **Be fruitful, and multiply, and replenish the earth, . . ."**

10. Deuteronomy 8:13 – <u>Belongings</u> = **Multiplied**
"And <u>when thy herds and thy flocks</u> **multiply,**
and <u>thy silver and thy gold</u> **is multiplied,** <u>and all</u>
that thou hast in multiplied."

Summary

It is a natural tendency to desire increase. Increase in wealth, increase in food, increase in friends, increase in health, and the list goes on according to your needs and wants.

Even nature has a desire and an instinct for increase. For to multiply in species or to generate countless, diverse seeds guarantees a continuum of life; otherwise, the beast or plant would end its existence and die. An increase is necessary for survival.

Thus, nature's living things automatically focuses not only on survival but also on increase. The same is with mankind. What we focus on the most is what we will get more of. Having a desire for more wealth or health, and we make an effort to multiply those desires without dwelling on the lack thereof, will expand to greater amounts for us.

Through the parable of the ten talents (see #1 above), we learn that increasing in wealth—or anything else of worth—is pleasing unto the Lord and almost expected. We need to increase in abilities in talents and knowledge. We grow that way, and then through achieving, we can help others do the same. We did not come to existence upon this miraculous earth just to stay the same and never grow or develop in spirit, abilities, or in making the effort to find our purpose and reach our potential. We expect the same with our own loved ones. We hope the best for them. To see them grow in strength and wisdom and service. Society needs their people to make a difference and to contribute talents and giving—that is how communities are enhanced, improve, and maintained. People with no desires for improvement or increase does not help themselves or others. They may actually become a problem that needs attention.

Increase is good. It is a want that makes life better and more fulfilled. But the positive end of increase results with the right side of thinking. Focus on what you want and not on what you don't want. Increase will manifest itself with the right ideas, the right thoughts, and the right actions. We need to become the best that we can be. To develop into the individual that contributes grows in godly character and makes a difference in the world. Increase is necessary to accomplish that ideal end.

Parable of Increase

Behold, at a fitness gym, there was a person working out with the thought of developing more muscle. The person was dedicated often throughout the week to lifting weights which built stronger muscles as time went on. An increase of muscle mass began to develop and appear. At the same time, this person developed an awareness and great interest in nutrition and how to cook healthy foods, thus in time becoming a sought-after chef specializing in fresh, organic menus. With an increase in skills, knowledge, and body health, the person was soon receiving an increase in compensation. Focusing on what the person loved brought much increase to their strength and income.

Photo credit: toridawnrector via Visual hunt / CC BY-SA

Every act, every deed of justice and
mercy and benevolence, makes
heavenly music in Heaven.

—Ellen G. White, 1827–1915

20. The Universal Law of Justice.

I am going to stretch this law somewhat to touch "Cause and Effect" as well as receiving justice for wrongs done to us as well as wrongs that need to be met in terms of the choices that we have made. There is a beginning and an end to most everything. The ball goes up, the ball come down. We do something or say something that is not appropriate or good, and we reap the result—or we pay the price. Justice is a law that has to be completed. "Result" is usually a more positive outcome, whereas "consequences" have a more serious connotation. No matter, the law has to be executed to complete the act. One cannot run from mistakes or misdeeds. They eventually will catch up to them at one time or another to be justly ended. [58AR]

Cause and Effect stretches from one extreme to another. From "I tripped over the hose and fell down" to "I shoplifted an article of clothing and now I am in jail." It is at this far end of "cause and effect" that the Law of Justice dwells in. When eternal laws are broken, prices have to be met, especially when dealing with man, not necessarily nature behaviors.

Wrongs from other people will be answered, but not necessarily by the one offended. God will perform justice as He sees necessary and right. Our job is to forgive, thus the Law of Forgiveness (see Chapter 14), but the Lord will take care of instances of justice. In fact, he paid the very high price of justice for our sake if we just repent and right our lives and actions. The act of the Atonement was to meet the ends of the given law. Alma 42:21–22 states,

And if there was no law given, if men sinned what could justice do, or mercy either, for they would have no claim upon the creature? But there is a law given, and a punishment affixed, and a repentance granted; which repentance, mercy claimeth; otherwise, justice claimeth the creature and executeth the law, and the law inflicteth the punishment; if not so, the works of justice would be destroyed, and God would cease to be God.

God is God and continues to be so forever, and he completes the justice of broken laws that we, His children, knowingly break. His act of love for all of us also includes helping make our weak selves stronger and our imperfect beings brighter. Jesus Christ's sacrifice for justice was truly heavy, heart-wrenching, and magnificent!

The Universal Law of Justice is forever present and demands fulfillment. If there is justice to be completed for crimes against us, we welcome it wholeheartedly, but it becomes much more uncomfortable if it is present for *us* to answer to. Thus, the moral of this law—for us—is to try and never break it if we don't want to answer to its demands of justice. Live the Golden Rule {59} "do unto others as you would have them do to you" and let justice fall on those who do not live this rule.

Justice will be met one way or another, but let God take that into his own hands and make that happen. We just need to make sure our lives are complete and performed with kindness, so when we meet our maker and we account for our life's actions, we will be at peace.

Blessings or Consequences in the Scriptures for the Universal Law of Justice

1. **Alma 42:15 – <u>Jesus</u> = Meet the Demands of Justice**

    And now, the plan of mercy could not be brought about except an atonement should be made; therefore <u>God himself</u> atoneth for the sins of the world, to bring about the plan of mercy, to appease the demands of justice, that God might be a perfect, just God, and a merciful God also.

2. **2 Nephi 2:7** – <u>Jesus Sacrifice</u> = **Answer the Law**
"**Behold, he** <u>offereth himself a sacrifice for sin,</u> **to answer the ends of the law, unto all those who have a broken heart and a contrite spirit; and unto none else can the ends of the law be answered.**"

3. **Mormon 3:14–15** – <u>Vengeance</u> = **Is Gods Action**
"**Behold the voice of the Lord came unto me, saying:**" <u>"Vengeance</u> **is mine, and I will repay: . . .**"

4. **Mormon 3:20** – <u>Humankind</u> = **Judged Before God**
And these things doth the Spirit manifest unto me; therefore I write unto you all. And for this cause I write unto you, that ye may know that <u>ye must all stand before the judgment-seat of Christ,</u> **yea,** <u>every soul who belongs to the whole human family of Adam;</u> **and ye must stand to be judged of your works, whether they be good or evil;**

5. **Ether 8:22–23** – <u>Wickedness</u> = **God Will Avenge**
And <u>whatsoever nation shall uphold such secret combinations,</u> **to get power and gain, until they shall spread over the nation, behold, they shall be destroyed; for the Lord will not suffer that the blood of his saints, which shall be shed by them, shall always cry unto him form the ground for vengeance upon them and yet he avenge them**

not. Wherefore, O ye Gentiles, it is wisdom in God that these things should be shown unto you, that thereby ye may repent of your sins, and suffer not that <u>these murderous combinations</u> shall get above you, which are <u>built up to get power and gain</u>—and the work yea, even the work of destruction come upon you, yea, even the sword of the justice of the Eternal God <u>shall fall upon you, to your overthrow and destruction</u> if ye shall suffer these things to be.

6. **D&C 107:84** – <u>None Exempt</u> = **From Justice**
   "Thus, <u>none shall be exempted</u> from the justice and the laws of God, that all things may be done in order and in solemnity before him, according to truth and righteousness."

7. **Jacob 6:10** – <u>Justice</u> = **Can Not Be Denied**
   "And according to the <u>power of justice, for justice</u> cannot be denied, . . ."

8. **2 Nephi 9:17** – <u>God's Law</u> = **Must be Fulfilled**
   "O the greatness and the <u>justice of our God! For he executeth all his words</u>, and they have gone forth out of his mouth, and <u>his law</u> must be fulfilled."

9. **Zechariah 7:9** – <u>Execute</u> = **True Judgment**
   "Thus speaketh the Lord of host, saying, <u>Execute</u> true judgment, and shew mercy and compassions every man to his brother;"

10. D&C 82:4 – Justice = Affixed to Law

Ye call upon my name for revelations, and I give them unto you; and inasmuch as ye keep not my saying, which I give unto you, ye become transgressors; and justice and judgment are the penalty which is affixed unto my law.

Summary

If there is anything that cries out for attention, it's the Law of Justice. It has to be met no matter what. It will not be missed or overlooked in the realm of Laws obeyed or disobeyed. Justice is the hammer of the law. It sounds its clang with authority and power. Some judgments are mild in redeeming restitution, others demand much more, depending on the heaviness of the error; however, size of the fixing should be in proportion to size of the mistake.

We are responsible for results or consequences in our lives; however, an enormous sacrifice was performed for our benefit so we would not have to pay for our mortal mistakes if we but repent. Jesus Christ suffered much to meet the demands of justice for laws broken by us. We need to praise His name and do all we can in appreciation of an act so tremendous in our behalf because of his great love for us. We do need to be aware that if we do not repent of mistakes done, then we will have to pay the demands of justice ourselves.

Broken laws demand an answering to, either right away or it will surface eventually to meet the consequences of justice. Some mistakes are minor and easy to straighten out, to repent of, or to redeem. Others require much more energy and action to right, depending on the extent of the law that was broken. The Law of Forgiveness (see Chapter 14) works with the Law of Justice, but only when everything is corrected and appeased. Only then can one start again and continue forward with peace of mind and heart.

Cause and Effect happens. We do or say things, and results or consequences develop automatically. We have no say in the outcome. We need to try our best to not pass judgment on others and do our best in living a positive uplifting life for ourselves and for others. We are mortals living in a mortal world and learning mistakes happen. They are a part of growing and developing. We just need to fix what went wrong and progress forward. Remembering that God is the one who passes judgment and makes sure the demands of justice is met. And He does that with much love and mercy on our part.

Life is a wonderment of joy and happiness mixed in the "learning experiences" that require correcting. Knowing that God loves us, helps us, guides us, but also lets us fail, get up, move forward, try again, make our own choices with consequence to pay or blessing to reap is a wonderful reassurance that His love is always with us—no matter what.

Parable of Justice

In the make-believe village called Anywhere, there are strings of lights that are hanging from poles that run throughout the village, keeping the village seeing and being able to produce. Like lines of colored Christmas lights, they give light to the town and bring joy to their hearts. When all the laws of the village are obeyed, then the bulbs stay on, and the village is happy and peaceful. But when a law has been disobeyed, then the lights immediately blink off until the wrong has been corrected and paid for by the offender or another who stands in their place. It is impossible for the lights to come on any other way. For justice has to be paid. Once the mistake is taken care of, then the lights bright up the village once more, and the people continue on with another peaceful, happy, productive day.

Photo credit: S@ndrine Néel via VisualHunt / CC BY-ND

Any fool can know. The
point is to understand.

—Albert Einstein

21. The Universal Law of Knowledge and Wisdom.

Certainly a city library does not even come close to what
is available to learn that is engrossed within the universe,
focusing on endless past happenings, to an eternity of future
facts, figures, and knowings that constantly change, producing more enlightenment to accumulate. Knowledge is
that which we can discover or understand or accumulate
from past happenings. Ways to attain knowledge ranges
from online sources, masses of book choices, classes at an
educational institution, talking to experts, and even pon-

dering our own thoughts mixed with prayer. We live in an ever-changing world with new gadgets, evolving theories and proofs, discoveries and experiences. One moment a discovery is supposed to change the difficulties of living or health, and then it may be tweaked because we found something else. However, knowledge that is eternally fact will never change, but just be more understood as our step-by-step learning process progresses. [60AR]

Even so, there is power that comes from accumulating knowledge and wisdom. It opens more opportunities that otherwise would not be available if we were not prepared. Gaining more understanding broadens the mind and opens it up to new possibilities, imaginations, and developments. Plus, it makes life more interesting when we study the hows, whys, wheres, and whens of things. Knowledge is also beneficial to a large measure when it comes to developing and enlarging our God-given gifts and talents. It is a learning process, a practicing process, and an enlightening process to master abilities.

Knowledge is valuable information that we can pass on to generations after us, as well as in our day-to-day communication from one person to another—a way to learn from someone who has already experienced an event instead of learning it the hard way ourselves. Wisdom is earned through past experiences of what to do or not to do the second time around (that is if we learned our lesson the first time). We do not need to "reinvent the wheel" over and over. To improve on its existence and functions, yes, but not to use up precious time reinventing the original thing over and over when it has already been created. That is not to say that present objects can't be manipulated, transformed, or updated. They certainly can and must be developed to keep up with modern devices and inventions. That is a definite reason why there needs to be a continuing desire to gain knowledge. It is a never-ending stream of energy that our minds need to keep up with and use in a developing world.

The scriptures are scattered with the advice to gain more knowledge and wisdom.

As a familiar verse in Proverbs (see #1 below) admonishes, "With all thy getting get understanding." And how do we attain understanding? Usually through our own experiences or taking the counsel from those who have experienced; however, just talking may need a push into understanding. One may need to ponder upon the information. Try to apply it into their lives and see how it may affect them. To understand may take some additional time to connect the dots and learn from what has been taught. No matter the source, wisdom usually comes with a certain amount of experience time. To understand the lesson the first time around is most desired.

The law of Wisdom is to have experienced, learned, and understood life's happenings—to learn from the past and applied that knowledge to the future and passed on that information to those who are just beginning. For knowledge is not necessarily understanding. You gain knowledge, but you experience wisdom. And with the gift of the Holy Ghost, we'll understand both.

Blessings or Consequences in the Scriptures for the Universal Law of Knowledge and Wisdom

1. **Proverbs 4:7** – <u>Knowledge</u> = **Understanding**
    "**Wisdom is the principal thing;** <u>therefore get wisdom</u>**: and with all thy getting get understanding.**"

2. **D&C 88:77–79** – <u>Gain Knowledge</u> = **In All Things**
    And I give unto you a commandment that you <u>shall teach one another the doctrine of the kingdom.</u>
    <u>Teach ye diligently</u> **and my grace shall attend you, that** <u>you may be instructed</u> **more perfectly in theory, in principle, in doctrine, in the law of the gospel, in all things that pertain unto the kingdom of God, that are expedient** <u>for you to understand;</u> **Of things both in heaven and in the earth, and under the earth; things which have been, things which are, things which must shortly come to pass; things which are at home, things which are abroad; the wars and the perplexities of the nations, and the judgments which are on the land; and a** <u>knowledge</u> **also of countries and of kingdoms—**

3. **D&C 88:118** – <u>Seek Wisdom</u> = **Out of the Best Books**
    "**And as all have not faith,** <u>seek ye diligently</u> **and** <u>teach one another words of wisdom;</u> **ea, seek**

ye out of the best books <u>words of wisdom; seek learning</u>, even by study and also by faith."

4. 3 Nephi 17:3 – <u>Ponder</u> = To Understand
    Therefore, go ye unto your homes, and <u>ponder upon the things which I have said,</u> and ask of the Father, in my name, that ye may understand, and <u>prepare your minds</u> for the morrow, and I come unto you again.

5. Moroni 10:3–5 – <u>Read, Ponder and Ask</u> = Truth of All Things
    Behold, I would exhort you that when ye shall <u>read</u> these things, if it be wisdom in God that <u>ye should read them,</u> that ye would remember how merciful the Lord hath been unto the children of men, from the creation of Adam even down until the time that ye shall receive these things, and <u>ponder it in your hearts.</u> And when ye shall receive these things, I would exhort you that ye would <u>ask God,</u> the Eternal Father, in the name of Christ, if these things are not true; and if <u>ye shall ask</u> with a sincere heart, with real intent, having faith in Christ, he will manifest the truth of it unto you, by the power of the Holy Ghost. And by the power of the Holy Ghost ye may know the truth of all things.

6. **D&C 130:19** – <u>Gain More Knowledge</u> = **Advantage after Life**

    "And if a person <u>gains more knowledge and intelligence in this</u> life through his diligence and obedience than another, he will have so much the advantage in the world to come.'

7. **D&C 89:19** – <u>Find</u> = **Treasures of Knowledge**

    "And shall <u>find wisdom</u> and great treasures of knowledge, even hidden treasures;"

8. **D&C 9:8** – <u>Study and Ask</u> = **Know if Right**

    But, behold, I say unto you, that you must <u>study it out in your mind; then you must ask</u> me if it be right, and if it is right I will cause that your bosom shall burn within you; therefore, you shall feel that it is right.

9. **Alma 32:34** – <u>Knowledge</u> = **Expands**

    And now, behold, is your knowledge perfect? Yea, <u>your knowledge</u> is perfect in that thing, and your faith is dormant; and this because you know, for ye know that the word hath swelled your souls, and ye also know that it hath sprouted up, that your <u>understanding</u> doth begin to be enlightened, and your mind doth begin to expand.

10. **Ether 3:19–20** – <u>Knowledge and Faith</u> = **Saw Jesus**

And because of the <u>knowledge</u> of this man he <u>could not be kept from beholding within the veil;</u> and he saw the finger of Jesus, which, when he saw, he fell with fear; for <u>he knew</u> that it was the finger of the Lord; and he had faith no longer, <u>for he knew, nothing doubting.</u> Wherefore, having this <u>perfect knowledge</u> of God, he could not be kept from within the veil; therefore he saw Jesus; and he did minister unto him.

Summary

The total of what can be learned or discovered equals the amount of knowledge that we attain. Additional information or imaginings are always within our reach through study and pondering. There is no end to knowledge and understanding through experiences that give us a higher level into wisdom—a realm of enlightenment. The more we seek new discoveries, principles, and light, the more power we will have being on a higher level of intelligence.

However, that is not to say that we are better than anyone else. It just means we have more understanding in our mind's eye. Everyone has learning and experiences. They may just be in a different domain than yours. More knowledge on certain subjects still gives one a greater advantage in that arena than another of lesser insight. Such as, training to be a doctor gives the medical student knowledge of medical things whereas a student in construction does not dwell on health subjects. Nonetheless, they are both knowledgeable about their passions of different employment.

The owl with the glasses that is supposed to represent being a wise fowl is an enjoyable symbol of life experiences that produce understanding. "The wise old owl" is mounted on a branch looking down at young students of existence and, with its large glasses, seeing possibilities of greatness, but also of making mistakes, failures in learning experiences, hard work, play, and love. {61}

It reminds me of the character of Merlin, the wizard, in *The Sword in the Stone* Disney animation movie. His dwelling is in a room high in the castle surrounded by mounds and piles of books everywhere. Large and small books on every subject that he pours over at his wooden desk accumulating vast amounts of knowledge and wisdom to advise to young Arthur, or anyone else. {62} Learning and knowledge is most important in giving us a more fulfilled life, but it must be mixed with faith and truth from God to be totally correct and right. God knows all. His is the true source of all that is right. Man studies and experiences and put together theories and ideas, but without the Holy Ghost and God by the student's side, ideas may fall short or be guesses that later on are discovered as incorrect statements. However, we are always learning, always progressing, always discovering new and interesting truths about our world and about ourselves—what a wonderful opportunity that is!

Parable of Knowledge/Wisdom

The accumulation of knowledge is like a person who is crossing a stream stepping on stones which they themselves must throw one at a time ahead into the flowing water. Another stone dropped into the stream presses him forward one step at a time. If no stones are dropped, then the person either stays where they are and eventually is swept away by the floods or has to turn around and go back, never progressing forward. A person has to continue always stepping forward by learning new things or is swept away or left behind from the floods of change and new technology.

Photo credit: Yukari* via Visual Hunt / CC BY-SA

Good works is giving to the poor and the helpless, but divine works is showing them their worth to the One who matters.

—Criss Jami

22. The Universal Law of Love (Unconditional).

All creatures were born with the capacity to love and the need to be loved. It is a feeling that touches the spirit and the soul, the whole of man. God created us because of great love for our being and becoming. The Lord Jesus Christ suffered for our sins and paid the price to meet the ends of the law because of His magnificent love for us. He was also the master of giving and spreading the natural need of love and belonging. Our souls were also created to share in the ever-encompassing throng of this tender emotion.

God's love has no bounds or exceptions for our soul. Some actions of man is not to be expected, but the soul of man is forever loved and longed to return back to Him. Like the love of parent to child, it is deep and entwining. From one individual to another, neighbor to neighbor, friend to friend, or even stranger to another unknown individual, our love should be unconditional without bounds. After all, we are all children of God which makes each and every one of us brothers and sisters in the Lord. Should we not try and understand another person and love them for what they can become and their godly created spirit. We all make mistakes. We all are learning, growing, and experiencing this worldly existence together. We can raise each other up to higher levels by showing tolerance, patience, and love to another human being that needs to do the same for us. As John 13:34 sweetly advises, "A new commandment I give unto you, that ye love one another; as I have loved you, that ye also love one another." [63AR]

Love is like the broth that soup is made of. Everything is supported and tasty within the herbal liquid that surrounds the ingredients. Love envelops everything in the universe. Everything worthwhile and good is created with love in mind. Love feels good. It kisses the soul and brightens the light in our eyes and puts a skip in our walk. Without the human touch of love, newborns die. Everyone is made to love and to receive love. It is the emotional base for our mortal existence. We yearn for it, to be accepted by others, and to be supported through life by love makes the goodness of life possible.

Unfortunately, some have learned to either not give love, or to give the wrong feelings that are similar to love, or to show their own kind of love in the wrong way—which is Satan's counterfeit of the emotion. True love is kind, unconditional, forgiving, and pure.

War is not love or kindness. Fighting or other negative low levels of emotion cannot support peace, love, and joy. Godly love is never a stab in the back, or an insult of words or actions, but of tenderness and acceptance. There should always be the spreading of love which dissolves all evil and builds up righteousness and charity. All Universal, eternal laws are supported and maintained by the heavenly emotion of love.

Blessings or Consequences in the Scriptures for the <u>Universal Law of Unconditional Love</u>

1. **John 3:16** – <u>God Loved the World</u> = **Gave His Son**
    "<u>For God so loved the world,</u> **that he gave his only begotten Son, that** <u>whosoever believeth in him</u> **should not perish, but have everlasting life.**"

2. **John 15:13** – <u>Give Life</u> = **For Friends**
    "Greater love hath no man than this, <u>that a man lay down his life for his friends.</u>"

3. **Leviticus 19:18** – <u>Love Neighbor</u> = **As Thyself**
    "<u>Thou shalt not avenge, nor bear any grudge</u> **against the children of thy people, but thou** <u>shalt love thy neighbour</u> **as thyself; I am the Lord.**"

4. **Mosiah 4:15** – <u>Serve and Love</u> = **One Another**
   "**But ye will teach them** <u>to walk in the ways</u> <u>of truth and soberness;</u> **ye will teach them to love one another,** <u>and to serve one another.</u>"

5. **Moroni 7:47** – <u>Charity</u> = **Pure Love of Christ**
   "**But** <u>charity</u> **is the pure love of Christ, and it** <u>endureth forever;</u> **and** <u>whoso is found</u> **possessed of it at the last day,** <u>it shall be well with him.</u>"

6. **Matthew 5:44** – <u>Love</u> = **Your Enemies**
   "<u>But I say unto you,</u> Love **your enemies,** <u>bless</u> <u>them</u> **that curse you,** <u>do good</u> **to them that hate you, and** <u>pray</u> **for them which despitefully use you, and persecute you;**"

7. **Deuteronomy 6:5** – <u>Love</u> = **The Lord**
   "<u>And thou shalt love</u> **the lord thy God** <u>with</u> <u>all thine heart, and with all thy soul, and with all</u> <u>they might.</u>"

8. **Ephesians 5:2** – <u>Christ</u> = **Loves Us**
   "**And walk in love,** <u>as Christ</u> **also hath loved us, and** <u>hath given himself</u> **for us an offering and a sacrifice to God for a sweet smelling savour.**"

9. **1 Corinthians 2:9** – <u>Great Things</u> = **To Those Who Love God**
   "**But as it is written,** <u>Eye hath not seen, nor</u> <u>ear heard, neither have entered into the heart of</u> <u>man, the things which God hath prepared</u> **for them that love him.**"

10. Romans 13:8 – <u>Love One Another</u> = **Fulfill Law**
"Owe no man any thing, but to <u>love one another: for he that loveth another</u> hath fulfilled the law."

Summary

The Universal Law of Unconditional Love acts just as it says, loving another person without judgment or expectations. It is an emotion that has no mission to change another person except to be a positive influence. This focuses on an exception of all humans no matter of culture, beliefs, or nationality. A brotherly love, not necessarily a romantic love—which has a place of its own.

The emotion of caring or loving also touches into the realms of appreciation for the earth and animals. Loving the beauties of the world and the innocents and wonders of other living things takes a place in our hearts as well as the affection we have for other people. Love connects to multiple strings that tug on our heart and brings us joy, laughter, and insights into the magnificent creations of God—including the love we have for natural, tasty, delicious food that He created for our pleasure and health.

Love is not a man-made emotion, but it is an eternal feeling that has always been. God created a wondrous, beautiful world because of his love for us. He blessed us with so much potential and gifts to use to produce a magnificent life with bounty and abundance surrounding us on all sides. Love has a power to transform, to uplift, and to cheer anyone at any time. We seek love and acceptance, and we give the same feelings to everyone, especially to the people we love most—our family and our God—unconditionally.

Love is sweet, and we all crave it—from birth to death. It is always present and establishes itself as a constant longing and accepting. A kiss on the cheek, a gentle hug, a "how are you" smile, or a word of uplifting praise are all small things that spread sunshine and cheer and love to others around us. It doesn't require a horde of people to fulfill that emotion, just a few individuals that touch our hearts and uplift our spirits. But no matter what, God will always shower us with unconditional love, knowing that fact helps calm that need and give peace to our spirits. "Love one another, as I have loved you" (John 13:34). The more we spread positive emotions of happiness, the more we receive ourselves, thus everyone is loved—touched with sweetness that uplifts us from day to day.

Parable of Unconditional Love

And, behold, there was a certain little child standing beside her mother behind the old-fashioned wooden counter at the town's country store gazing wide-eyed at the many jars filled with sweet candies that lined the wall in front of them. "I love the red and yellow ones best," exclaimed the little girl, pointing her finger at them. "I also love the orange and purple ones!" added the excited child. "I thought you loved the red and yellow ones best?" asked her mother. "No, I love them all no matter what color they are, they are all my favorite?" replied the child matter-of-factly. And so it is with people, we should love them all—as God does.

Photo credit: Beverly & Pack via Visual Hunt / CC BY

Obedience brings success; exact
obedience brings miracles.

—Russell M. Nelson

23. The Universal Law of Obedience.

No other law means anything or even exists properly unless
the Universal Law of Obedience is followed and applied.
The universe is not going to manipulate its established cycles
and rhythms of physics unless the elements follow the course
of their assigned functions. Nature automatically follows its
laws of purpose—its inherent programming that was created
by God. Nature obeys its assigned commands instantly and

without negotiating or arguing. A star is not going to say to its maker, "I'm not going to glow today because I am tired of being hot, plus I'd rather be a tree." The wonders of nature consistently obeys its creator and fulfills its purpose in time and space. [64AR]

Now, mankind, on the other hand, is born with the choice to obey laws or not to follow rules that were made for his benefit and blessing. Agency is an eternal law that man had the gift of long before coming to mortal existence. Am I going to choose to follow an established law this time or ignore the law and take what may?

First we need to be aware of universal, eternal, and God-given laws to make a choice of whether to follow them or not. However, the interesting fact remains that the laws do not wait till you are aware of them for them to function, they are constantly and consistently in motion no matter if we realize it or not. So the sooner we become aware of laws in our lives and the blessings they form, the better it is to make choices that make our lives better because we chose to follow them rather than fight them, even if it's unknowingly.

The earth is not going to stop being round even though humans thought it was flat. Or the Law of Divine Oneness isn't going to start when someone finally realizes that there is energy around everything and that we all came from God. The energy fact is always there and goes on and on if a person understands it or not. Since we are constantly living one law or another, it is beneficial to our happiness the sooner we understand the laws and discover which ones we are skimping on or need to put a greater effort into obeying—so we can reap the blessings from following it. That is the whole purpose of having laws to begin with. They are for our safety, security, love, progression, and growth. Where there is a law, there is also a blessing or a benefit for following that law. {65}

In fact, the first law of Heaven is obedience. It is also a way to show our love to our Lord. Similar to children showing respect and love toward their parents by following righteous established house rules and the things that they say or ask of them. How can we progress without obeying the eternal laws that God has given us in our life's manual— the scriptures. The earth obeyed its formation to become a beautiful, functional place for mankind to come to, to live out our existence and reach our potential by choosing to obey the laws that were created before we even came to earth.

Many important Universal Laws are a part of our everyday lives, and when we make positive choices to obey these laws, the better and happier and more fulfilled our lives will be. For an example, if we want more health, then we need to understand and obey the laws that welcome better health. (And I don't think junk food and manipulated foods are a part of that.) If more abundance is desired by us, then we need to follow the Universal Law of Abundance. It is as plain as that. If you want the blessing, then obey the law. Obedience opens the door to possibilities and many amazing blessings.

Blessings or Consequences in the Scriptures for the Universal Law of Obedience

1. **D&C 130:20–21** – Obey Law = **Reap Blessings**
   There is a law, irrevocably decreed In heaven before the foundations of this world, **upon which all blessings are predicated—**
   And when we obtain any blessing from God, it is by obedience to that law upon which it is predicated.

2. **Abraham 4:18** – Elements = **Obeyed to Form Earth**
   "And the Gods watched those things which they had ordered **until they obeyed."**

3. **D&C 89:18** – Obey Law = **Health**
   "And all saints who remember to keep and do these sayings, walking in obedience to the com-mandments, **shall receive health in their navel and marrow to their bones;"**

4. **Moses 5:5** – Adam = **Obeyed God**
   And he gave unto them **commandments, that they should worship the Lord their God, and should offer the firstlings of their flocks, for an offering unto the lord. And** Adam **was obedient unto the commandments of the lord.**

5. **D&C 59:3** – Obey = **Blessings**
   "Yea, blessed are they whose feet stand upon the land of Zion, who have obeyed my gospel; for they

<u>shall receive</u> **for their reward the good things of the earth, and it shall bring forth in it's strength."**

6. **Alma 57:21 –** <u>Obey</u> **= Mothers and Leaders**
   Yea, and <u>they did obey and observe to perform every word of command with exactness;</u> **yea, and** <u>even according to their faith it was done unto them;</u> **and I did remember the words which they said unto me that their mothers had taught them.**

7. **1 Nephi 3:7 –** <u>Go and Do</u> **= Lord Will Help**
   And it came to pass that I, Nephi, said unto my father: <u>I will go and do the things which the Lord hath commanded,</u> **for I know that the Lord giveth no commandments unto the children of men, save he shall prepare a way for them that they may accomplish the thing which he commandeth them.**

8. **John 15:10 –** <u>Keep Commandments</u> **= Abide in Love**
   "If ye <u>keep my commandments,</u> **ye shall abide in my love; even as I have kept my Father's commandments, and abide in his love."**

9. **Joshua 24:24 –** <u>God's Word</u> **= Obey**
   "And the people said unto Joshua, The Lord our God will we serve, <u>and his voice</u> **will we obey."**

10. **Ephesians 6:1–2 –** <u>Children</u> **= Obey Parents**
    <u>"Children,</u> **obey your parents in the Lord: for this is right." "Honour thy father and mother;"**

Summary

In order to gain anything worthwhile, one must obey the procedure or law that requires certain actions to manifest its blessings. A high level of achievement follows applying the action of study and persistence. Accomplishments don't just happen without following specific rules to employ for the desired outcome. Even the universe, nature itself, continues its life cycles because of laws that always existed without question or pause.

The Universal Law of Obedience must be practiced religiously for progression to happen. Our own potential is only achieved by following specific and precise laws that direct the way toward that goal. Shortcuts around laws do not produce the same results, or even results that one would want. To obtain certain blessings, then following or applying certain laws are a must in order to acquire the blessing. Similarly to a child receiving an award or treat after completing a certain job or behavior. Do the job, get the reward, no ifs, ands, or buts.

However, it is very calming to know that when obedience is chosen, rewards or blessings will follow. God does not take back His promises or blessings when His laws are precisely followed. But God also answers obedience in His own time for our best benefit and blessing. Patience is a virtue that both man and nature must apply through their development and progression. Remember, obedience is the first law of Heaven to achieve the highest level of mortal and eternal life. {66}

Parable of Obedience

Once upon a cloudy day, there was a certain driver of a car traveling down a country road. Thinking that they knew best, they ignored the warning signs posted alongside the road as they speed past. Signs that read "Slow Around the Corner" or "Slick When Wet" or "Watch for Animal Crossing."

The rain began to fall causing the road surface to become slick. "I've got this, no problem," foolishly said the driver. Soon the car was out of control, missing the corner and sliding to a stop just in front of a few frightened deer that were about to bound across the road. The disturbed driver drove differently after that.

Photo credit: brewbooks via Visualhunt / CC BY-SA

Our character is basically a composite of
our habits. Because they are consistent,
often unconscious patterns, they
constantly, daily, express our character.

—Stephen Covey, 1932–2012

24. The Universal Law of Patterns/Habits.

Beautiful fabric designs that are repeated over and over
again has the same idea as habits of people that repeat
themselves day in and day out. It doesn't take into account
if the habit patterns are good or not so good. They just are.
Patterns appear everywhere from rings flowing out from
a pebble dropped in water to the number of peddles in
a flower. Patterns not only include habit repetitions, but
specific designs in nature that repeat themselves according

to how they were created to form. Like a garment pattern purchased to lay out on fabric to create a set dress or shirt and then used again to create the same clothing piece over and over, only the colors and textures may change. [67AR]

The amazing blueprints of individual buds, leaves, or feathers were delicately conceived before the world was formed. Patterns from a minute scale to huge earth covering clouds of the same formation and type. We have a way of missing or overlooking nature's repetitions of design because we either take them for granted or because the wondrous pattern is too small to notice without kneeling down and examining it up close.

Cycles of nature are also patterns. Patterns of living and dying, sowing and reaping, becoming and developing. However, I think of patterns more of repetition of designs placed in formation that duplicates itself over and over, never changing unless interrupted by the creator for a purpose.

Habits that repeat themselves over and over because of programming in the subconscious mind never change either unless a desire, an awareness, and a successful resolution changes the habit pattern. Nothing is impossible or set in stone, but dedicated effort is required to transform an old habit by introducing a new one. An everyday commitment to apply the new desired way of doing things finally replaces the old over a fair amount of time. Habits are not necessarily good or bad, it just depends on the result of the action. If the outcome is for the improvement and worthy functioning of life or if the pattern is detrimental and deteriorating to the individual.

Dysfunction habit patterns can be dissolved by doing something different over a long period of time, thus the "different" thing becomes the regular habit pattern. Repentance from addictive habits or from any other harming pattern can be overcome by desire, assistance, and strength from a loving Heavenly Father. Worthy, righteous, and kind habit patterns are the ones we want to hold on to and continue performing. Adding more of those kinds of repetitions into our lives makes for a more meaningful and potential achieved existence.

Blessings or Consequences in the Scriptures for the Universal Law of Patterns

1. **Exodus 25:9** – <u>After the Pattern</u> = **Make It**
    "**According to all that I shew thee,** <u>after the pattern</u> **of the tabernacle,** <u>and the pattern</u> **of all the instruments thereof, even so shall ye make it.**"

2. **1 Chronicles 28:11–12** – <u>Pattern</u> = **To Solomon's Temple**
    The David gave to Solomon his son the <u>pattern of the porch, and of the houses thereof, and of the treasuries thereof, and of the upper chambers thereof, and of the inner parlours thereof, and of the place of the mercy seat,</u> **And the** <u>pattern of all that he had by the spirit, of the courts of the house of the Lord, and of all the chambers round about, of the treasuries of the house of God, and of the treasuries of the dedicated things:</u>

3. **Titus 2:7** – <u>Pattern</u> = **Good Works**
    "**In all things** <u>shewing thyself a pattern</u> **of good works: in doctrine shewing uncorruptness, gravity, sincerity,**"

4. **D&C 97:10** – <u>Build a Temple</u> = **Using a Pattern**
    "**Verily I say unto you, that it is my will** <u>that a house should be built</u> **unto me in the land of Zion, like unto the pattern which I have given you.**"

5. **D&C 102:12** – <u>Pattern</u> = **To Speak First**
    Whenever a high council of the church of Christ is regularly organized, according to <u>the foregoing pattern, it shall be the duty of the twelve councilors to cast lots by numbers, and thereby ascertain</u> **who of the twelve shall speak first,** <u>commencing with number one and so in succession to number twelve.</u>

6. **Moses 6:46** – <u>Pattern</u> = **For Book of Remembrance**
    "For a book of remembrance <u>we have written among us, according to the pattern</u> **given by the finger of God; and it is** <u>given in our own language."</u>

7. **Helaman 15:7** – <u>Belief Pattern</u> = **Can Change**
    And behold, ye do know of yourselves, for ye have witnessed it, <u>that as many of them as are brought to the knowledge of the truth, and to know of the wicked and abominable traditions of their fathers, and are led to believe the holy scriptures, yea, the prophecies of the holy prophets, which are written, which leadeth them to faith on the lord, and unto repentance, which faith and repentance</u> **bringeth a change of heart unto them—**

8. **D&C 50:24** – <u>Continue in God</u> = **Receive More Light**
    "That which is of God is light; and <u>he that receiveth light, and continueth in God,</u> **receiveth**

more light; and that light groweth brighter and brighter until the perfect day."

9. **D&C 94:1–2 –** <u>Pattern</u> **= To Build City of Zion**
   That ye shall commence a work of laying out and preparing a beginning and foundation of the city of the stake of Zion, here in the land of Kirtland, beginning at my house. And behold, it must be <u>done according to the pattern which I have given unto you</u>**.**

10. **D&C 88:42–45 –** <u>Pattern Law</u> **= Planets and Times and Seasons**
    And again, verily I say unto you, <u>he hath given a law unto all things,</u> **by which they move in their times and their seasons; And their courses are fixed, even the courses of the heavens and the earth, which comprehend the earth and all the planets. And they give light to each other in their times and in their seasons, in their minutes, in their hours, in their days, in their weeks, in their months, in their years—all these are one year with God, but not with man. The earth rolls upon her wings and the sun giveth his light by day, and the moon giveth her light by night, and the stars also give their light, as they roll upon their wings in their glory, in the midst of the power of God.**

Summary

Repetition is the foundation of patterns. Nature is full of designs that multiply themselves or repeat themselves over and over again to form a complete creation. A certain number and shape of petals that form a delicate flower, always the same in that species. Patterns that appear on windblown dunes or the exact same number of leaves on a green, curly fern. Patterns are beautiful and precise and predicable. Designs that are used for construction of an object, or designed, precut tissue paper pieces that are pinned onto fabric to construct a garment, are also patterns. Manufactured bolts of material that has colorful, imaginative images on them that repeat themselves continuously are beautiful patterns to see and feel.

The pattern of certain behaviors become regular habits that are performed willingly or subconsciously. Habits can be positive and uplifting such as the habit of addressing with a pleasant salutation as you pass by someone or the habit of giving your children a hug before they go to bed. However, patterns of actions can also be detrimental and harming.

Additional habits that only bring the owner poor health and an inability to control self. Or the habit of not wearing a protective car seatbelt or the habit of eating a big bowl of ice cream before you retire for the night. Any undesirable pattern of behavior in our life can be transformed or replaced by better actions with a dedicated, different new action that is repeated again and again with support from others who care and with plenty of patience.

Actions that we do or say over and over on a regular, predictable manner are patterns in our lives. Righteous repetitions are desirable and are for the betterment of the individual and uplifting to others. All good actions are from God, who yearns for worthy behaviors on our part. The habit of nightly prayers or attending a place of worship on the Sabbath are all worthy and uplifting patterns of righteous living. An awareness of how we automatically respond or behave throughout our day helps determine if we are owning progressive patterns or our behaviors need to be changed, tweaked into new patterns that benefit us.

Parable of Patterns

And, behold, there came a certain townsfolk that walked the same path to and from his destination every day on schedule. His boots strolled the same winding walkway, past the same shops, tipped his hat to the same storekeepers through the window, smiled at other townsfolk as he passed by, patted the same dog that wagged its tail, stepped in the same mud puddle without notice, bought the same meal at the vendor stand, returned back home at the same time, tripped in the same puddle, wiped off his boot with the same handkerchief (from the same pocket), smiled at the familiar townsfolk, picked up his mail in the same box by his gate, removed his worn boots, hugged his family waiting on the porch, went inside his comfortable home, and shut the door. Regular and familiar—but never experiencing different ways, things, or places.

photo credit: reXraXon via Visualhunt.com / CC BY

What good is the warmth of
summer, without the cold of
winter to give it sweetness.

—John Steinbeck, 1902–1968

25. The Universal Law of Polarity.

Polarity deals with the opposite ends of things, situations, and ideas. There is nothing that does not have an opposite. Black–white, up–down, small–large, good–bad, and so forth. Even nature had its opposites of day and night, growing or wilting and pure, clear stream water versus silt laden and mucky water. If we are in a position that we do not care for, then we can move or change to the other end of the spectrum where we are more joyous and comfortable. Of course, any change does not manifest its opposite immediately, desire and action bring about change. [68AR]

Life experiences have a way of announcing their polarity because of their effect on ourselves. If we have a bad hair day, then we appreciate a great, uplifting day of everything going right. Or we have experienced rudeness on the road while driving, but then appreciate a driver that lets us enter a lane first in front of them. The same idea flows with touching something hot that burned your skin and quickly learning to avoid that situation again. It is interesting also that as Will Smith relates, the feeling of "bliss is on the other side of fear." {69} When we are afraid of performing or doing something out of our comfort zone, we need to realize that achievement is on the other end—far away from fear. Fear of failure. Fear of success. Low confidence to change or do something different from what we usually, comfortably do all require a change in order to flee from these stresses.

Will Smith, the actor, once said, "God placed the best things in life on the other side of terror! Everything that you want is on the other side of fear and on the other side of your maximum fear, are all of the best things in life." So if we want to achieve great, meaningful things or reach to a higher level of being—which is extending ourselves in realms that are unfamiliar but necessary—we need to swing from the common place of fear to the brighter end containing bliss, wonder, and extreme joy.

It is a blessing that there are opposites of everything. For then we are aware that whatever we are experiencing that we do not enjoy, then there is always the other end of the situation to turn around and shoot for. Opposite ends are always available, they are always a choice. The Universal

Law of Cause and Effect is also in play here. It is this law that gets you where you want to go or become because of the effort and actions we administer to attain the desired results that we are seeking. Do I want to have abundance or lack? Do I want love or loneliness or spiritual uplifting or hone a feeling of spiritual lowness and loss? God's eternal law of agency gives us the opportunity and ability to make whatever choice we desire—at whatever end of the spectrum you desire to be in.

Some opposites reveal themselves quickly and others develop as time goes on. For example, burnt toast versus lightly browned bread happens in minutes, whereas mismanaged health practices that over time develop into illness or disease. Being aware of choices place us immediately or in the future where we want to be or may direct our path in the opposite direction. The Law of Polarity is evident in all we do and dwells in nature continually. We just need to decide which end of things we want to be at.

Blessings or Consequences in the Scriptures for the Universal Law of Polarity

1. **2 Nephi 2:11** – <u>Opposition</u> = **In All Things**

     For it must needs be, that <u>there is an opposition in all things</u>**. If not so, my first-born in the wilderness, righteousness could not be brought to pass, neither wickedness,** <u>neither holiness nor misery, neither good nor bad</u>**. Wherefore, all things must needs be a compound in one; wherefore, if it should be one body it must needs remain as dead,** <u>having no life neither death, nor</u>

corruption nor incorruption, happiness nor misery, neither sense nor insensibility."

2. **2 Nephi 2:15–16** – First Parents = **Agency to Choose**

   And to bring about his eternal purposes in the end of man, after he had created our first parents, **and the beasts of the field and the fowls of the air, and in fine, all things which are created, it must needs be that there was an opposition; even the forbidden fruit in opposition to the tree of life; the one being sweet and the other bitter. Wherefore, the Lord God gave unto man that he should act for himself. Wherefore, man could not act for himself save it should be that he was enticed by the one or the other.**

3. **Alma 42:16–18** – Opposite Law = **Punishment**

   Now, repentance could not come unto men except there were a punishment, **which also was eternal as the life of the soul should be,** affixed opposite to the plan of happiness, **which was as eternal also as the life of the soul. Now, how** could a man repent except he should sin? **How could he sin if there was no law? How could there be a law save there was a punishment? Now, there was a punishment affixed, and a just law given, which brought remorse of conscience unto man.**

4. Moses 6:55–56 – Bitter = Sweet

    And the Lord spake unto Adam, saying: Inasmuch as the children are conceived in sin, even so when they begin to grow up, sin conceiveth in their hearts, and they taste the bitter, that they may know to prize the good. And it is given unto them to know good from evil; wherefore they are agents unto themselves, and I have given unto you another law and commandment.

5. 2 Nephi 2:27 – Liberty = Captivity

    Wherefore, men are free according to the flesh; and all things are given them which are expedient unto man. And they are free to choose liberty and eternal life, through the great Mediator of all men, or to choose captivity and death, according to the captivity and power of the devil; for he seeketh that all men might be miserable like unto himself.

6. D&C 58:4 – Tribulations = Blessings

    "For after much tribulation come the blessings. Wherefore the day cometh that ye shall be crowned with much glory; the hour is not yet, but is nigh at hand."

7. D&C 122:7 – Hardships = Blessings and Experience

    And if thou shouldst be cast into the pit, or into the hands of murderers, and the sentence of death passed upon thee; if thou be cast into the deep; if the billowing surge conspire against thee;

if fierce winds become thine enemy; if the heavens gather blackness, and all the elements combine to hedge up the way; and above all, if the very jaws of hell shall gape open the mouth wide after thee, **know thou, my son, that all these things shall give thee experience, and shall be for thy good.**

8. **Isaiah 1:19–20 –** Obedient **= Or Rebellious**
    "If ye be willing and obedient, **ye shall** eat the good of the land: **But if ye refuse and rebel, ye shall be devoured with the sword; for the mouth of the Lord hath spoken it."**

9. **Genesis 3:22, 24 –** Man Knows Good **= And Know Evil**
    And the lord God said, Behold, the man is become as one of us, to know good **and evil; and now, lest he put forth his hand, and take also of the tree of life, and eat, and live for ever; So he drove out the man; and he placed a the east of the garden of Eden, Cherubims, and a flaming sword which turned every way, to keep the way of the tree of life.**

10. **Isaiah 1:18 –** Sin, Red **= Repentance, White**
    "Come now, and let us reason together, saith the Lord: through your sins be as scarlet, **they shall be as white as snow;** though they be red like crimson, **they shall be as wool."**

Summary

The Universal Law of Polarity exists in everything. Happy/ Sad, Left/Right, Long/Short, He said/She said; this list could go on and on when you contemplate all things mortal and in nature. Knowing both ends of the spectrum can give you choices. If you don't enjoy where you are at now, then make the attempt to change and move to another area of whatever is not going right. If you desire to get out of financial lack and to move to the other end of means, which is to have more wealth, then develop yourself, learn how to grow wealth, manage wealth, think wealth, give wealth, and wealth will manifest itself because you were focused on the law of increase instead of attracting lack.

Opposites are interesting in the fact that they are so different in their function and meaning. Somewhere in the middle is what is referred to as the "gray" area, which wobbles back and forth in the center toward one end or the other. Extremes are maneuvering from the total end of the stick to the other opposite end without stopping in between. Such as, from all engulfing or paralyzing fear of speaking in front of a large crowd to no fear whatsoever, thus talking to people becoming one of your favorite activities to do. It is said that when you do the thing you fear, that fear will melt away—and you will be at the opposite end emerged in energizing bravery.

It is refreshing to have polarity around us. I'm sure one would get tired of always having the sun shining and never either setting or cloud covered expecting rain. A warm spring emerging from a cold winter or welcoming a night of sleep after a busy, hectic day. It is also soul lifting to be able to fix mistakes and repent versus housing in guilt and dismay. God always gives us choices to make on our own of which end of life we want to dwell in or develop. Agency to decide every day concerning our actions and thoughts, if to be positive or negative, to be kind or ornery or to express love and gratitude or complain and be selfish. Opposites exists continually and constantly in our mortal living and among the wonders of nature. To make an effort to stop and analyze consequences and outcomes plays a big part of which end of the spectrum of things we magnetize to, which becomes our life.

Parable of Polarity

Two orchard farmers grew different fruits. One farmer grew sour yellow lemons which made his face twist into a puckered look whenever he tasted them. But they were necessary. The other farmer grew sweet red strawberries which brought a twinkle and a smile to his face whenever he tasted them. They were necessary too. That is all they knew, because that is all they produced. One day, they met at the market each carrying a basket of their own harvest. "Your fruit is a different color than mine," said one farmer. "Why does your face pucker so when you bite in your yellow fruit?" inquired the other. Each sampled the fruit from the other farmer's basket. "Oh, now I know why you smile so, this red fruit is so sweet—I never knew!" smiled the once frowning farmer. The other wrinkled his nose and laughed. They now knew the bitter from the sweet, and they were both necessary.

photo credit: chefranden via Visual Hunt / CC BY

It's not hard to decide what you want your life to be about. What's hard is figuring out what you're willing to give up in order to do the things you really care about.

—Shauna Niequist

26. The Universal Law of Sacrifice.

This particular law has multiple feelers that connect into natural life and self-improvement. For new seedlings to emerge and gain a life of their own, they must replace the existing older crop—a death or a sacrifice of life for new life to thrive. The comings and goings of life being born and dying, Cycles and Rhythms, Sacrifices or giving up the out-of-date or older life or procedures for new life, new ideas, and new visions. [70AR]

Sacrifices can come in the form of giving up time for something else or giving up some sleep to accomplish a goal. For self-improvement, it may be giving up another activity to get skill in another. Such as, giving up free time to practice piano, or giving up leisure time to lift weights and exercise. Basically, the Law of Sacrifice is giving up something for something better. It is the only way to progress and improve. To give up time to study to have more career choices, to give up an old habit for a more favorable one, or even to resolve sins to become more spiritual and whole.

We are always making choices of one kind or another of "I'll give you this if you give me that." Seems everything has a price or an exchange possibility to get something else.

The Law of Sacrifice is not always necessarily bad or hurting or difficult. It just depends on the situation, the need, and the desire. Giving up time is not necessarily hard to do, but it may be required, and it can either be welcomed and agreed to sacrifice with good intentions and attitudes or it can be irritating and annoying. But then, sacrificing is a personal decision and one that is not usually made without a willingness to give up—to get. If you admire someone that has talents or skills that you wished you had, then you need to sacrifice the time and energy to do what it requires to get those sought-after abilities. The person who has developed them had to do the same thing.

There is a spiritual side of the Law of Sacrifice that deals with a repentant person giving up their sins to get closer to God. Or giving up time to serve, as well as willingly giving or donating 10 percent of income to obey the Law of Tithing. {71} Sacrificing our time, talents, and possessions to help others in need is exchanging our maybe selfish tendencies for a more caring and giving personality. To obey the Lord requires giving up things or ideas that do not develop divine attributes. Laws of God are only designed to improve mankind and, when applied, help return us back to live with him. In order to progress and become our best self, we must sacrifice things, habits, or ideas that do not service or direct us in that direction.

Of course, the ultimate sacrifice was the one Jesus Christ gave because of his love for us so that we could repent and live again. His offering of himself gave us the ability to repent and not pay the price—for Jesus took that debt and paid it himself to meet the Law of Justice, but only if we choose to use that gift and be forgiven.

Relationships with loved ones require choices that will help bond connections more solidly. To spend more time or attention requires a sacrifice of giving or rescheduling our own time to create a more happier, unified home life or couple relationship. The Law of Sacrifice is a forever rotating action. To become better, we much replace the ineffective. To improve, we must develop better habits and give up the old. To lift higher in spirit, we must give up negativism and disbelief. To reach more of our potential, we must give up or sacrifice what is keeping up stuck or comfortable and extend our reach higher. Nature sacrifices the worn and dying for the new and living. If we don't keep improving, we may start going backward, staying in one spot only causes a person to sacrifice a better existence or life. They may be sacrificing the wrong thing.

Blessings or Consequences in the Scriptures for the Universal Law of Sacrifice

1. **D&C 59:8** – Sacrifice to God = **Broken Heart and Contrite Spirit**
   "**Thou shalt** offer a sacrifice unto the Lord thy God **in righteousness even that of a broken heart and a contrite spirit.**"

2. **Hebrews 7:27** – Sacrifice = **Jesus Offered Himself**
   "**Who needeth not daily, as those high priest, to** offer up sacrifice, **first for his own sins, and then for the people's: for this he did once, when he offered up himself.**"

3. **Hebrews 13:15–16** – Sacrifice = **To Do Good and Give Praise to God**
   By him therefore let us offer the sacrifice **of praise to God continually, that is, the fruit of our lips giving thanks to his name. But to do good and to communicate forget not: for with** such sacrifices God is well pleased.

4. **2 Nephi 2:7** – Jesus's Sacrifice = **Meet Justice**
   "**Behold, he** offereth himself a sacrifice for sin, **to answer the ends of the law, unto all those who have a broken heart and a contrite spirit; and unto none else can the ends of the law be answered.**"

5. **D&C 59:12** – <u>Offer Up</u> = **Oblations/Sins**
    "But remember that on this, the Lord's day, thou <u>shalt offer</u> thine oblations and thy sacraments unto the Most High, confessing thy sins unto thy brethren, and before the Lord."

6. **D&C 64:23** – <u>Sacrifice Money</u> = **Pay Tithing**
    "Behold, now it is called today until the coming of the Son of Man, and verily it is a <u>day of sacrifice</u> and a day for the tithing of my people, . . ."

7. **D&C 132:50** – <u>Sacrifice</u> = **To Obey**
    Behold, I have<u> seen your sacrifices, and will forgive all your sins; I have seen your sacrifices</u> in obedience to that which I have told you. Go, therefore, and I make a way for your escape, as I accepted the offering of Abraham of his son Isaac.

8. **Hebrews 13:15** – <u>Offer Up</u> = **Praise**
    "By him therefore let us <u>offer the sacrifice</u> of praise to God continually, that is, the fruit of our lips giving thanks to his name."

9. **D&C 26:1** – <u>Devote Time</u> = **To Study**
    "Behold, I say unto you that you shall <u>let your time be devoted</u> to the studying of the scriptures, ..."
    Ervin/Laws/180

10. D&C 88:124 – <u>Sacrifice</u> = **To Become Better**
<u>Cease</u> to be idle; <u>cease</u> to be unclean; <u>cease</u> to find fault one with another; <u>cease</u> to sleep longer than is needful; retire to they bed early, that ye may not be weary; arise early, that your bodies and your minds may be invigorated.

Summary

Throughout ancient history, sacrifices were of killing the innocent or the submitting of live offerings of firstborn animals to God or idols. The Law of Sacrifice (that I am focusing on) dwells not upon these definitions, but of letting go and becoming better. Of giving up the used and old to develop the young and new. In this interpretation, sacrifice is something positive and cultivating.

To become more spiritual in nature, we need to give up actions that are opposite of righteousness and the divine. Sacrificing time or bad habits or sins brings us closer to God and his blessings. The Lord, Jesus Christ, paid the price of justice by giving up his own body and spirit for us so that we could become better by repenting and receiving power to improve ourselves. The Law of Sacrifice has a strong spiritual side to it that lifts our soul and strengthens our weaknesses.

By giving up or sacrificing things or actions that keep us in a rut of common or insufficiency, we give ourselves the ability to progress and achieve. Time and play is sacrificed to be skilled at playing an instrument through practicing on a daily basis. To achieve excellent grades in education, a student needs to sacrifice activities that takes away the time to study. Any good advancement of self requires sacrificing the old self's habits to improve. The Law of Sacrifice is to give up something that keeps us down in order to become or get something better or of higher value. If there is no sacrificing, there is no improving.

Parable of Sacrifice

Behold, there were five accomplished people. One person played the flute magnificently, sending the most heavenly tones to the listening ear. The second was a master teacher, speaking wisdom and truths to many students. The third performed expertise skills to damaged, hurting, or sick patients. The fourth was strong in muscle and fit in endurance. The last person of the five gave up bad habits and then helped others do the same. How did these five individuals become so wonderful and amazing? Through sacrificing their time to become who they wanted to be or do what they wanted to do.

Photo credit: professor.jruiz via VisualHunt.com / CC BY

Your life is like a puzzle, and only God
know what the end result will look like.
Let him put the pieces together.

—Anonymous

Chapter 4

I've got Law Puzzle Pieces Everywhere . . . Now to Put Them All Together to Find That Our Big Picture is Truly Amazing and Magnificent

Laws of all kinds surround our daily comings and goings, ins and outs and arounds and throughs. Our lives are pieced together by them if we realize it or not. The Universal Law of Cause and Effect, for example, pronounces results from the simplest of actions on up to the larger consequence from mistakes that we make as well as wonderful manifestations as the result of positive choices—from which fruit to buy to which educational institution to attend or not.

Laws govern how we respond to others, how we feel around them (their energy and vibrations), or if we believe in what they tell us through conversation to how much we believe in our own abilities to perform anything. Natural Laws of the Universe give us the opportunity to either shovel snow, carry an umbrella, or wear a hat to shade our eyes from the glowing sun. And then, because of eternal laws, we can either count our many blessings of abundance or focus on lack, depending on what we want to attract into ourselves and into our lives. Laws are part of living, breathing, and existing. If you believe that fact or not, it will never change.

Laws originate from nature, from God, or from man. Reasons for laws vary from running the universe to the development and outcome of our souls and spirits to where we park our car or how much taxes we need to pay each year. Different laws rule different reasons and phases of our lives. No matter which laws we choose to obey or not will determine how happy and fulfilled our life will become. Proverbs 29:18 advises, "But he that keepeth the law, happy is he."

The issues of trouble and chaos in our lives or that exists from others choices are results of broken, disobeyed, or ignored obedience to following any law. Stealing or lying are defying the laws of peace, love, and faith, which will then ricochet off with the demands of Justice. Partaking of junk food or laziness brakes the important Law of Health and Action, which produces ill health, sickness, and loss of achievement. Anything that is manifesting itself for good or ill is the result of obeyed or broken laws.

Happiness and peace are the outcome of followed laws. War, hatred, and violence are the consequences of broken or dismantled laws of man and mishandled Laws of God. However, Universal Laws and Laws of God are eternal and will never change. Even through the rights of agency, our choices will still be for positive or negative, which then shows obedience or disobedience to given laws. Eternal laws do not create problems, only man does that through his own thinking and actions. However, man's law can be for the good or ill of the people, depending on the hearts of those who have created them.

Thus, we see that eternal and righteous laws or rules produce a high level of living—one in peace, love, and productivity. By obeying Universal and God's laws that were designed for the benefit of all living creatures and things of nature, subsequently can only manifest blessings and progression. Good to good, right to right, heavenly to the eternal. One can only go backward by ignoring the laws of God that were created and written by his hand. The city of Enoch, recorded in the Bible, rose up to the heavens to dwell with God. Why? Because those who dwelt within obeyed completely the laws taught to them. Laws of kindness, Laws of love, Laws of Giving and Receiving, and Laws conditioning them to return back to God. Laws such as Repentance, Baptism, Forgiveness, and Charity. Through God's grace, He will help us reach our greatness.

Righteous Laws are beautiful and divine. They are designed to bring out the best in our hearts, mind, and spirit. When we apply them into our everyday actions, we come and go in a high level of frequency, which connects with others to produce the same happy state. God lives in a place of security and love, and we can too by obeying Universal and God's laws that exist in feelings of divine oneness, beauty, and wisdom.

By continually seeking eternal knowledge, improving our natural, God-given talents and abilities, and striving for Christ-like living, we will touch the lives of others by helping them reach their potential as well. Life is magnificent! Our abundance is without question! And our spirits can soar above any evil if we only obey the Universal and

Laws of God—which were designed just for us mortals in this glorious world that has such high potential of peace, love, and joy. Think it, feel it, and share it.

Blessings and promises go hand in hand with living eternal laws. Each law has a condition and a blessing or promise attached. Without question, if you obey a law, there will automatically be a blessing produced back to you. It may be immediate or will manifest in God's time, but you *will* receive the outcome that results in obedience. Guaranteed!

As the scripture teaches in D&C 130:20–21,

There is a law, irrevocably decreed in heaven before the foundations of this world, upon which all blessings are predicated— And when we obtain any blessing from God, it is by obedience to that law upon which it is predicated.

Certain blessings are attained by obeying certain laws and only through obedience to that law can they be given. We also much remember that we cannot be saved or receive blessings if we do not know or acknowledge Universal and God's eternal laws. D&C 131:6 advises, "I is impossible for a man to be saved in ignorance."

We must know the laws to advance, to progress, and to reach a saving place in the hereafter. It is a comfort to realize that everyone will have the opportunity to gain knowledge in this subject to be able to make a choice.

God also absolutely states, "I, the Lord, am bound when ye do what I say; but when ye do not what I say, ye have no promise" (D&C 82:10). It is as simple as that—obey and be blessed or choose not to obey and not receive any blessing. I, for one, hope that we all pause a moment in our busy lives and observe where our lives are going and which laws are going well for us and which we need to obey a little better. This world is amazing and wonderful! And our lives can be just as glorious and fulfilling if only we obey the laws that are eternal and that God has created for our benefit and happiness. Now let's put all the law pieces together and form a fantastic picture that shows the wonders of our potential, our health, our good associates, our creativity, and our love for God and all living things. Let's make our efforts, small or large, count toward as many blessings as we can accumulate for the betterment of ourselves, our families, and our friends—simply by following eternal laws.

D&C 3:5: "Behold, you have been entrusted with these things, but how strict were your **commandments;** and remember also the **promises** which were made to you, if you did not transgress them." It is marvelous indeed to understand the laws and blessings that abound for our benefit in achieving the most that we can attain and enjoy during our mortality upon this resplendent earth of nature's delights. We must have an attitude of patience, enjoy the journey, and with a willingness to service God—not necessarily for the blessings themselves, but because we want to. Because our gratitude and love for all good things.

Like Santa's Christmas bag that is filled to the rim with delicately wrapped presents just waiting to generously tumble out toward us when we are "good." Universal Laws mixed with God's laws entwined and highlighted the eternal, great teachings in the scriptures, gives us all the guidance we need for a most satisfying life—that is if we choose to obey!

photo credit: professor.jruiz via VisualHunt.com / CC BY

Life is a series of experiences, each
one of which makes us bigger, even
though sometimes it is hard to realize
this. For the world was built to develop
character, and we must learn that the
setbacks and grieves which we endure
help us in our marching onward.

—Henry Ford, 1863–1947

Chapter 5

Bonus Chapter—Well, Wait a Minute, What about a Law about Endurance?

An action that keeps popping up in my mind—but one that I have yet to discover that is actually labeled as the Law of Endurance—which is an action that requires an individual to "come to the end" or to "endure through thick or thin whatever it takes" to achieve a desired project, goal, or life purpose. Perhaps you could call it Sow and Reap or the Law of the Harvest, but I think it should entail much more than that. It is an act of never quitting till you are completely and utterly finished and done, ended, crossed the finish line, kaput!

God strongly encourages us to "endure to the end." So many scriptures refer to this counsel such as, "and if they *endure* (italicized for emphasis) unto the end they shall be lifted up at the last day, and shall be saved in the everlasting kingdom of the Lamb;" (1 Nephi 13:37), or "whoso repenteth and is baptized in my name shall be filled; and if he **endureth** to the end, behold, him will I hold guiltless before my Father at that day when I shall stand to judge the world" (3 Nephi 27:16), or in D&C 121:29:, "All thrones and dominions, principalities and powers, shall be revealed and set forth upon all who have **endured** valiantly for the gospel of Jesus Christ." These are only a few of the references that the all-important action of a sticking-it-out-to-the-end law applies.

Life is a time to learn, to enjoy, to share, but it is also a time to advance in character, in faith, and in obedience. Blessings await us in the eternities for those who endure well, repent and right wrongs, make an effort to live as Jesus would and forgive. Living our daily lives can be joyous and challenging, but enduring to the end of life has great rewards. As the thirteenth Article of Faith declares, "We believe all things, we hope all things, we have *endured* many things, and hope to be able to *endure* all things . . ." (**Italicized** for emphasis). Life isn't over till we pass on, so enduring isn't over till that moment arrives as well.

The act of enduring flows over into all facets of life happenings; from finishing a grade level in school and then graduating from a higher educational institution, to finishing a race without quitting, to enduring a boring talk or lecture, from carrying out an assigned responsibility, to completing a goal that takes months to reach to its tail end. Enduring is the action that truly accomplishes advancement and blessings. Falling short before the end arrives does not bring fulfillment and only manifests discouragement and may stimulate a habit of "quitting too soon" and never finishing or accomplishing anything worthwhile.

Growing nature and living creatures, for the most part, complete their earthly mission or purpose all while enduring demanding elements or opposing foes that either force them to become stronger or exposes their weaknesses.

Trials for all of nature and man require a "living through" or an endurance to survive and thrive. Living plants and trees endure the swirls of high winds, fierce blizzards, or scorching sun. Mankind endures trials of temptations, job loss, injuries and diseases, war and famine (to name a just a few). But to endure and keep trying and applying determination produces a new job, healed wounds, better health, peace, and food sources. Enduring trials with a positive mind and a willing heart for something better opens up the mind to new discoveries or improved ways of doing things, but one needs to "keep at it" to continue forward with a better future in mind, to overcome and get over hurdles and setbacks, and to solve without ceasing.

To finish anything, one needs to keep going till anything is done, over, or complete. An action of enduring is required, either with a willing heart and positive attitude or perhaps with boldness and determination accompanied with sweat and tears. The view is at the top of the mountain with the work or struggle being the journey. As God has said, blessings await for those that endure to the end. May we all keep enduring to completion whatever our goals and dreams may be and to journey through our lives with joy, determination, and fulfillment—to accumulate the blessings and rewards of obedience and endurance.

Parable of Endurance

There once was a certain determined man who only was focused on his dream of reaching the top of the rugged mountain. Day after day, he envisioned himself reaching his goal. His friends said that they would join him, but along the steep trek up the rocks, one decided to hike to the nearby lake, another got too many text messages that needed to be answered, and another thought it was too difficult and went back down. None, except the dreamer, saw the magnificent horizon nor felt the swelling of joy from his accomplishment—taking one step at a time, enduring to the end, or rather the top!

Endured To
The End

References and Additional Reading

Quote References { # }, Additional Reading [AR] (listed below);

{1} Genesis 3.

{2} ElRay L. Christiansen, "The Laws of God Are Blessings,"
—(General Conference, April 1975).

{3} Bruce R. McConkie, Mormon Doctrine, p. 395

[3AR] Additional Reading for Laws.

[4AR] Additional Reading for Laws.

{5} an old Medieval Proverb quote

https://www.quora.com/What-is-the-origin-of-the-phrase-this-too-shall-pass

{6} First law of Thermodynamics (3 laws of Thermo-dynamics–Boundless.com)

"Law of Conservation of Mass" – (Chemistry)

A law that states that mass cannot be created or destroyed; it is merely rearranged. https://www.boundless.com/chem-istry/textbooks/boundless-chemistry-textbook/atoms-molecules-and-ions-2/history-of-atomic-structure-32/the-law-of-conservation-of-mass-194-3698/

[7AR] Additional Reading for the Law of Abundance.

{8} Luke 6:4-7

{9} Matthew 14:14–21

{10} – Joseph B. Wirthlin, "The Abundant Life," – (Ensign, May 2006).

{11} – President James I. Faust, "The Abundant Life," (Ensign, Nov. 1985).

[12 AR] – Additional Reading for the Law of Action.

[13 AR] Additional Reading for the Law of Attraction/ Vibration.

[14AR] Additional Reading for the Law of Association.

{15} – Scripture Connections:

* 2 Timothy 2:26: "And that they may recover themselves out of the snare of the devil, who are taken captive by him at his will."

*Alma 12:6: "And behold I say unto you all that this was a snare of the adversary, which he has laid to catch this people, that he might bring you into subjection unto him, that he might encircle you about with his chains, that he might chain you down to everlasting destruction, according to the power of his captivity."

[16AR] Additional Reading for the Law of Association and Law of Attraction.

[17AR] Additional Reading for the Law of Attraction.

{18} Pyramid of Vibrations – (more sources on images)

http://www.hearts-expanding-allow-love.com/2012/02/03/how-to-raise-your-energetic-vibration/

[19AR] Additional Reading for the Law of Belief.

{20} Watty Piper, *The Little Train That Could*, original (Platt & Munk Publisher), Newer versions available.

[21AR] Additional Reading for the Law of Belief.

[22AR] Additional Reading for the Law of Cause and Effect.

[23AR] Additional Reading for the Law of Cause and Effect.

[24AR] Additional Reading for the Law of Change.

[25AR] Additional Reading for the Law of Command.

{26} Mark 11:23–24: "And shall not doubt in his heart, but shall believe that those things which he saith shall come to pass; he shall have whatsoever he saith."

[27AR] Additional Reading for the Law of Command.

[28AR] Additional Reading for the Law of Creation.

{29} 7 Natural Laws of the Universe – Law of Gestation, https://gittefalkenberg.wordpress.com/2010/02/28/the-7-natural-laws-of-the-universe/

{30} Animal Cloning - http://www.understandinganimal-research.org.uk/how/areas- research/animal-cloning/

{31} Walking Robots - http://engineering.tamu.edu/research/2012/walking-robots

[32AR] Additional Reading for the Law of Cycles and Rhythms.

{33} See #5

{34} Plan of Salvation or Plan of Happiness. https://www.lds.org/bc/content/ldsorg/content/english/ manual/missionary/pdf/36950_the-plan-of-salvation-eng. pdf?lang=eng

[35AR] Additional Reading for the Law of Divine Oneness.

{36} http://energyfanatics.com/2015/09/08/energy-fields-auras-do-they-interact-with-mind-matter/-Energy Fields & Auras, by Pao Chang, Photos using a Kirlian Camera.

{37} Clinton Ober, Stephen T. Sinatra, MD, and Martin Zucker, *Earthing* (Published by Basic Health Publications, Inc. – 28812 Top of the World Drive, Laguna Beach, CA 92651 – 2010).

[38AR] Additional Reading for the Law of Faith.

[39AR] Additional Reading for the Law of Fellowship.

{40} – 3 Nephi 1:27

[41} – *Our Heritage: A brief History of The Church of Jesus Christ of Latter-day Saints*, "Chapter 7: Establishing an Ensign to the Nations," pg 81 (Published by The Church of Jesus Christ of Latter-day Saints).

[42AR] Additional Reading for the Law of Forgiveness.

[43AR] Additional Reading for the Law of Choice.

{44} Universal Law #4 – 'Law of Choice' -http://www. coachingandleadership.com/blog/universal-law-4-the-law-of-choice-we-have-the-power-to-choose/

[45AR] Additional Reading for the Law of Giving and Receiving.

{46} President Thomas S. Monson, An Attitude of Gratitude", (Feb. Ensign, 2000).

[47AR] Additional Reading for the Law of Gratitude.

{48} Hymns of the Church of Jesus Christ of Latter-Day Saints, "Count Your Blessings" pg. 241 Text by Johnson Oatman Jr. (1856–1922) (Published by The Church of Jesus Christ of Latter-Day Saints).

{49} D&C 59:21: "And in nothing doth man offend God, or against none is his wrath kindled, save those who confess not his hand in all things, and obey not his commandments."

{50} Colossians 3:17: "And whatsoever ye do in word or deed, do all in the name of the Lord Jesus, giving thanks to God and the Father by him."

[50AR] Additional Reading for the Law of Gratitude.

[51AR] Additional Reading for the Law of Health.

{52} D&C 89: (Word of Wisdom)

{53} Thomas S. Monson, "In Quest of the Abundant Life," Ensign March 1988.

{54} Genesis 1:27

{55} #21 above

[56AR] Additional Reading for the Law of Increase.

{57} Elder Franklin D. Richards, "The Law of Abundance" Ensign June 1971, (Journal of Discourses, vol. 11, pg 119, mentioned in his talk).

[58AR] Additional Reading for the Law of Justice.

Ervin/Laws/195

{59} Matthew 6:12: "Therefore all things whatsoever ye would that men should do to you, do ye even so to them: for this is the law and the prophets."

[60AR] Additional Reading for the Law of Knowledge and Wisdom.

{61} By an anonymous poet,

"A wise old owl sat in an oat;

The more he saw the less he spoke;

The less he spoke the more he heard;

Why can't we all be like that wise old bird?"

{62} From the Disney movie *Sword in the Stone* (1963)— Merlin's room of books image-*http://www.awaltz-throughdisney.com/uploads/6/2/7/6/6276678/4644600_orig.jpg*

[63AR] Additional Reading for the Law of Unconditional Love.

[64AR] Additional Reading for the Law of Obedience.

{65} D&C 130:20–21

{66} William D. Oswald, Second Counselor in the Sunday School General Presidency, "Obedience: The First Law of Heaven"(Ensign, January 2008).

[67AR] Additional Reading for the Law of Patterns.

[68AR] Additional Reading for the Law of Polarity.

{69} From a Will Smith interview.

https://www.youtube.com/watch?v=0DNv2p2ayZ0

[70AR] Additional Reading for the Law of Sacrifice.

{71} Numbers 18:26, 3 Nephi 24:8, D&C 119:4

Additional Reading Information Per Law; Introduction of Laws -

[3AR] "Principles with a Promise" - A Theodore Tuttle (speeches.buy.edu), January 31, 1978 Devotional

[4AR] Justin Perry, *I Wish I Knew This 20 Years Ago* (Published by YouAreCreators, Inc., 2014) "On Changing Your Frequency/Mood," pg.32.

Anne E. Angelheart, *Twelve Universal Laws* (Published by Balboa Press, a Division of Hay House–1663 Liberty Drive, Bloomington, IN 47403, 2011), "Chapter 2: The Law of Energy or Vibration," pg 9.

1. Law of Abundance –

[7AR] Venice Bloodworth, *Key To Yourself* (Published by DeVorss & Company – P.O. Box 550, Marina del Rey, CA 90294 – originally in 1952, renewed 1980) Chapter 10: – "Faith," pg 51.

Vic Johnson, *You Become What You Think About* (Published by Laurenzana Press – P.O. Box 1220, Melrose, FL 32666 – 2014) Chapter 1: "Cause and Effect" #4 "Focusing on Lack Instead of Abundance," pg 9.

2. Law of Action -

[12 AR] Wallace D. Wattles, *The Science of Getting Rich* (Published by Barnes & Noble – The Barnes & Noble

Library of Essential Reading – originally in 1910, this addition 2007) Chapter 12 – "Efficient Action," pg. 55.

Herbert Harris, *The Twelve Universal Laws of Success* (Published by the LifeSkill Institute, Inc. – P.O. Box 302, Wilmington, NC 28402 – September 2006) Chapter 7: "The Universal Law of Action," pg. 117.

Anne E. Angelheart, *Twelve Universal Laws* (Published by Balboa Press, a Division of Hay House – 1663 Liberty Drive, Bloomington, IN 47403 – 2011), Chapter 3: "The Law of Action," pg 21.

3. Law of Association -

[14AR] Ashley Fern, Why You Are the Company You Keep" Elite Daily, http://elitedaily.com/life/why-you-are-the-company-you-keep/ 'Law of Association' - www.freelifeways.org/welcome/about-us/the-50-spiritual-laws.., #23

Chris Crowe, "Good by Association" –– (New Era, May 1990).

[16AR] Additional Reading for the Law of Association and Law of Attraction.

Raymond Holliwell, *Working with the Law* by (Published by BN Publishing – info@bnpublishing.com or www.bnpublishing.com, 2008) Chapter 4: "Law of Attraction," pg. 39.

4. Law of Attraction -

[17AR] Additional Reading for the Law of Attraction.

Anne E. Angelheart, *Twelve Universal Laws* (Published by Balboa Press, a Division of Hay House – 1663 Liberty Drive, Bloomington, IN 47403, 2011) Chapter 7: "The Law of Attraction," pg 45.

[13 AR] Chapter 2: "The Law of Energy of Vibration," pg. 9.

Raymond Holliwell, *Working with the Law* (Published by BN Publishing, info@bnpublishing.com or www.bnpublishing.com, 2008) Chapter 4: "Law of Attraction," pg 39.

*Other Sources of Knowledge: Bob Proctor, T. Harv Eker, John Assaraf (websites/Youtube).

5. The Law of Belief

[19AR] Adam Sicinski, "The Universal Law of Belief," iqmatrix.com/law-of-belief.

[21AR] Bob Proctor, "The Subconscious Mind," "Understanding the Power of Paradigms," Youtube.com/user/BobProctorTV,

Venice Bloodworth, *Key To Yourself* (Published by DeVorss & Company – P.O. Box 550, Marina del Rey, CA 90294, originally in 1952, renewed 1980) Chapter 4: "The Subconscious Mind," pg 21.

6. The Law of Cause and Effect

[22AR] Vic Johnson, *You Become What You Think About* (Published by Laurenzana Press – P.O. Box 1220, Melrose, FL 32666, 2014) Chapter 1: "Cause and Effect," pg 5.

Deepak Chopra, *The Seven Spiritual Laws of Success* (Co-published byAmber-Allen Publishing and New World Library – P.O. Box 6657, San Rafael, CA 94903, 1994) Chapter 3: "The Law of Cause and Effect," pg 37.

Anne E. Angelheart, *Twelve Universal Laws* (Published by Balboa Press, a Division of Hay House – 1663 Liberty Drive, Bloomington, IN 47403, 2011) Chapter 5: "Law of Cause & Effect," pg 35.

[23AR]   Raymond Holliwell, *Working with the Law* (Published by BN Publishing – info@bnpublishing. com or www.bnpublishing.com, 2008) Chapter 7: "The Law of Compensation," pg 66.

Bob Proctor, "11 Forgotten Laws' – Law of Compensation" (Proctor & Gallagher Institute) – Youtube.com/watch?v=mm4NZShgZ-U

7. <u>**Law of Change -**</u>

[24AR]   Herbert Harris, *The Twelve Universal Laws of Success* (Published by the LifeSkill Institute, Inc., P.O. Box 302, Wilmington, NC 28402, September 2006) Chapter 2: "The Universal Law of Change," pg. 53.

8. <u>**Law of Command**</u>

[25AR]   Herbert Harris, *The Twelve Universal Laws of Success* (Published by the LifeSkill Institute, Inc., P.O. Box 302, Wilmington, NC 28402, September 2006) Chapter 4: "The Law of Command," pg 83.

Venice Bloodworth, *Key To Yourself* (Published by DeVorss & Company, P.O. Box 550, Marina del Rey, CA

90294, originally in 1952, renewed 1980) Chapter 30: "The Power of Word," pg 126.

[27AR] Venice Bloodworth, *Key To Yourself* (Published by DeVorss & Company, P.O. Box 550, Marina del Rey, CA 90294, originally in 1952, renewed 1980) Chapter 6: "Ideas and Affirmation," pg 30.

Vic Johnson, *You Become what You Think About* (Published by Laurenzana Press, P.O. Box 1220, Melrose, FL 32666, 2014) Chapter 5: "The Power Within Yourself," Become a Self-Fulfilling Prophecy, pg 62.

9.   The Law of Creation-

[28AR]   "Universal   Law   of   Creation,".api.ning. com/.../**105UniversalLaws**.pdf - #64

10. Law of Cycles and Rhythms.

[32AR]   Anne E. Angelheart, *Twelve Universal Laws* (Published by Balboa Press, a Division of Hay House, 1663 Liberty Drive, Bloomington, IN 47403, 2011) Chapter 11: "The Law of Rhythm," pg 71.

Christin Sander, "Metaphysical Laws| The Twelve Universal Laws Explained in a Nutshell," The Law of Rhythm, https://exemplore.com/magic/12 universal laws,

Tania Kotsos, "The Seven Universal Laws Explained," The Law of Rhythm, http://www.mind-your-reality.com/ seven universal laws.html – Mind Your Reality –

*"The Law of Cycles,"_Posted by SevanBomar, "105 Universal Laws," #15, http://www.resistance2010. com/forum/topics/105-universal-laws

11. <u>Law of Divine Oneness</u>

[35AR] Justin Perry, *I Wish I Knew This 20 Years Ago* (Published by YouAreCreators, Inc., 2014) "On Being Connected and Divine Order," pg. 63.

Anne E. Angelheart, *Twelve Universal Laws* (Published by Balboa Press, a Division of Hay House, 1663 Liberty Drive, Bloomington, IN 47403, 2011) Chapter 1: "The Law of Oneness," pg 1.

Christin Sander, "Metaphysical Laws |the Twelve Universal Laws Explained in a Nutshell,"The Law of Divine Oneness, https://exemplore.com/magic/12_universal_laws –

12. <u>Law of Faith</u> -

[38AR] Venice Bloodworth, *Key To Yourself* (Published by DeVorss & Company, P.O. Box 550, Marina del Rey, CA 90294, originally in 1952, renewed 1980) Chapter 10: "Faith," pg. 51.

Justin Perry, *I Wish I Knew This 20 Years Ago,* "On Strengthening Your Faith to Attract Bigger Things," (Published by YouAreCreators, Inc.) pg 127.

13. <u>Law of Fellowship</u> -

[39AR] Dick Sutphen, *Lighting the Light Within* (Published by Valley of the Sun Publishing, Box 38, Malibu, CA 90265, August 1987) Chapter 13: "The Twenty Primary Universal Laws," #13 "The Law of Fellowship," pg. 116.

14. Law of Forgiveness -

[42AR] Lonnie C. Edward. M.D., *Spiritual Laws That Govern Humanity and the Universe* (Published by the Grand Lodge of the English Language Jurisdiction, AMORC, Inc., 1342 Naglee Avenue, San Jose, CA 95191, 2011) Chapter 7: "Forgiveness and the Indwelling Soul," pg 61.

Herbert Harris, *The Twelve Universal Laws of Success* (Published by the LifeSkill Institute, Inc., P.O. Box 302, Wilmington, NC 28402, September 2006) Chapter 12: "The Universal Law of Truth" "The principle of forgiveness," pg 184.

Raymond Holliwell, *Working with the Law* (Published by BN Publishing, info@bnpublishing.com or www.bnpublishing.com, 2008) Chapter 9: "Law of Forgiveness," pg 83.

15. Law of Choice

[43AR] Dick Sutphen, *Lighting the Light Within* (Published by Valley of the Sun Publishing, Box 38, Malibu, CA 90265, August 1987) Chapter 13: "The Twenty Primary Universal Laws," #8 "The Law of Free Will," pg 114.

16. The Law of Giving and Receiving

[45AR] Justin Perry, *I Wish I Knew This 20 Years Ago* (Published by YouAreCreators, Inc., 2014) "On Giving," pg 40.

Deepak Chopra, *The Seven Spiritual Laws of Success* (Co-published by Amber-Allen Publishing and New

World Library, PO Box 6657, San Rafael, CA 94903, 1994) Chapter 2: "The Law of Giving," pg 25.

Bob Proctor, "Law of Receiving" from the "11 Forgotten Laws," https://www.youtube.com/watch?v=KbHgBOEVMcY

17. Law of Gratitude -

[47AR] Dick Sutphen, *Lighting The Light Within* (Published by Valley of the Sun Publishing, Box 38, Malibu, CA 90265, August 1987) Chapter 13: "The Twenty Primary Universal Laws," #12 "The Law of Gratitude," pg 116.

Justin Perry, *I Wish I Knew This 20 Years Ago* (Published by YouAreCreatorsInc., 2014) "On Gratitude," pg 87.

[50AR] "Lesson 34: "Prayer, Precious and Powerful" - The Presidents of the Church: Teacher's Manual, 1996, https://www.lds.org/manual/the-presidents-of-the-church-teachers-manual/lesson-34-prayer-precious-and-powerful?lang=eng&_r=1

18. Law of Health -

[51AR] "Word of Wisdom," D&C 89.

"Disease Prevention," Harvard T.H. Chan – School of Public Health – https://www.hsph.harvard.edu/nutritionsource/disease-prevention/ "The Eight Universal Laws of Health" – from "The Ministry of Healing" by E. G. White, pg. 127, Living Manna Ministries http://www.modernmanna.org/modern-manna-media/health-articles/8-laws-of-health/

Jane Birch *Discovering the Word of Wisdom* (Published by Fresh Awakenings)

David Wolfe, *Superfoods* (Published by North Atlantic Books)

19. Law of Increase -

[56AR] Wallace D. Wattles, *The Science of Getting Rich* (Published by Barncs & Noble, The Barnes & Noble Library of Essential Reading, originally in 1910, this addition 2007) Chapter14: "The Impression of Increase," pg 64.

Raymond Holliwell, *Working with the Law* (Published by BN Publishing, info@bnpublishing.com or www.bnpublishing.com, 2008) Chapter 6: "Law of Increase," pg 59.

Bob Proctor, "11 Forgotten Laws," The Law of Increase, *https://video.search.yahoo.com/yhs/ search;_ylt=AOLEVvUX3YdZCyYAHI8Px Qt.;_ylu=X3oDMTByMDgyYjJiBGNvbG- 8DYmYxBHBvcwMyBHZ0aWQDBHNlYwN- zYw--?p=11+forgotten+laws+proctor+law+of+in- crease&fr=yhs-elm-001&hspart=elm&h- simp=yhs-001#id=3&vid=dfa59f912ab5b329e- 37fe16744e2f894&action=view*

20. Law of Justice

[58AR] Elder dalin H. Oaks, "The Demands of Justice" (Alma 42:22–25) LDS Media Library, https://www. lds.org/media-library/video/2012-08-2440-the-de- mands-of-justice?lang=eng,

21. Law of Knowledge and Wisdom -

[60AR] *Justin Perry, I Wish I Knew This 20 Years Ago (Published by YouAreCreators, Inc., 2014) "On Knowledge and Fear," pg 105.*

22. Law of Unconditional Love -

[63AR] Herbert Harris, *The Twelve Universal Laws of Success* (Published by the LifeSkill Institute, Inc., PO Box 302, Wilmington, NC 28402, September 2006) Chapter 9: "Harmonic Relationship with Other People," pg 149.

Dick Sutphen, *Lighting the Light Within* (Published by Valley of the Sun Publishing, Box 38, Malibu, CA 90265, August 1987) Chapter 13: #17 "The Law of Unconditional Love," pg 118.

Lonnie C. Edward. M.D., Spiritual Laws That Govern Humanity and the Universe (Published by the Grand Lodge of the English Language Jurisdiction, AMORC, Inc., 1342 Naglee Avenue, San Jose, CA 95191, 2011) **Chapter 4: "Creating Peace and Unconditional Love," pg 33.**

23. Law of Obedience -

[64AR] Raymond Holliwell, *Working with the Law* (Published by BN Publishing, info@bnpublishing.com or www.bnpublishing.com, 2008) Chapter 11: "Law of Obedience," pg. 97.

24. *Law of Patterns*

[67AR] *"The Law of Patterns" #66, "105 Universal Laws" posted by Sevan Bomar, http://www.resistance2010.com/ forum/topics/105-universal-laws – Law of Patterns.*

25. Law of Polarity

[68AR] Anne E. Angelheart, *Twelve Universal Laws* (Published by Balboa Press, a Division of Hay House, 1663 Liberty Drive, Bloomington, IN 47403, 2011) Chapter 10: "The Law of Polarity," pg 65.

Justin Perry, *I Wish I Knew This 20 Years Ago* (Published by YouAreCreators, Inc., 2014) "On the Law of Polarity," pg 125.

26. Law of Sacrifice -

[70AR] Raymond Holliwell, *Working with the Law* (Published by BN Publishing, info@bnpublishing. com or www.bnpublishing.com – 2008) Chapter 10: "Law of Sacrifice," pg 90.

Universal Laws – photos
(Visual Hunt) and quotes

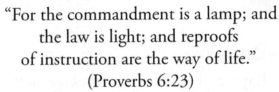

Introduction – planet -
Photo via VisualHunt
"For the commandment is a lamp; and
the law is light; and reproofs
of instruction are the way of life."
(Proverbs 6:23)

1. <u>**Law of Abundance – helicopter seeds – my own**</u>
<u>**photo**</u>

"Honour the Lord with thy
substance, and with
the first fruits of all thine increase;"
"So shall thy barns be filled with plenty, and thy
presses shall burst out with new wine."
(Proverbs 3:9–10)

2. Law of Action - Worker on roof -

Photo credit: The Library of Congress via VisualHunt
"The desire accomplished is sweet to the soul . . ."
(Proverbs 13:19)

3. Law of Association – Eagle heads -

Photo credit: Eric Kilby via Visual hunt / CC BY-SA
"Associate yourself with men of good quality
if you esteem yourself own reputation. It is
better be alone than in bad company."
(George Washington, 1732–1899)
http://www.quotationspage.com/quote/2397.html

4. Law of Attraction – Magnet and balls -

Photo credit: Philippe Put via Visual Hunt / CC BY

Mind is the Master power that moulds and makes,
And Man is Mind, and evermore he takes The tool of
Thought, and, shaping what he wills, Brings forth a

thousand joys, a thousand ills:—He thinks in secret, and
it comes to pass: Environment is but his looking-glass.
(James Allen, 1864–1912)
http://www.notable-quotes.com/a/allen_james.html

5. <u>Law of Belief – Field and barn -</u>

Photo credit: TumblingRun via
Visualhunt.com / CC BY-ND

"Therefore I say unto you, what things
soever ye desire, when ye pray, believe that ye
receive them, and ye shall have them."
(Mark 11:24)

6. <u>Law of Cause and Effect - Worn rocks -</u>

Photo credit: toddwendy via VisualHunt / CC BY
Ervin/Laws/207

"Every thought is a course and every condition is an effect.
Change your thoughts and you change your destiny."
(Joseph Murphy, 1898–1981)
http://www.azquotes.com/author/19461-Joseph_Murphy

7. <u>Law of Change - Chameleon -</u>

Photo credit: Michael-H-Photography via VisualHunt.com

"When we are no longer able to change a situation,
we are challenged to change ourselves."
(Victor Frankl, 1905–1997)
http://www.azquotes.com/author/5121-Viktor_E_Frankl

8. <u>Law of Command - Planet -</u>

Photo credit: Prairiekittin via VisualHunt / CC BY-ND

"There is great force hidden in a gentle command."
(George Herbert, 1593–1633)
https://www.brainyquote.com/quotes/
quotes/g/georgeherb152904.html

9. <u>Law of Creation – Meadow and mansion -</u>

Photo credit: steffen# via VisualHunt / CC BY-ND
Ervin/Laws/208

"Imagination is the beginning of creation. You imagine what you desire, you will what you imagine and at last you create what you will."
(George Bernard Shaw, 1856–1950)
https://www.brainyquote.com/quotes/
quotes/g/georgebern113045.html

10. <u>Law of Cycles and Rhythms</u> – <u>Water falls -</u>

Photo credit: Ian Sane via VisualHunt.com / CC BY

"Man appears for a little while to laugh and weep, to work and play, and then to go to make room for those who shall follow him in the never-ending cycle."
(Aiden Wilson Tozer, 1897–1963)
https://www.brainyquote.com/quotes/quotes/a/
aidenwilso403033.html?src=t_cycle

11. <u>Law of Divine Oneness – Man and child by ocean</u> --

Photo credit: Natalia Medd via VisualHunt / CC BY

> "Quantum physics thus reveals a basic
> oneness of the universe."
> (Erwin Schrodinger, 1887–1961)
> https://www.brainyquote.com/quotes/
> quotes/e/erwinschro304795.html

12. <u>Law of Faith – Person on mountain top</u>

Photo credit: Paxson Woelber via Visual Hunt / CC BY

> "Faith is to believe what we do not see,
> and the reward of this faith is to see what we believe."
> (Saint Augustine, ad 354–430)
> https://www.brainyquote.com/quotes/
> quotes/s/saintaugus121380.html

13. <u>Law of Fellowship – Hands</u>

Photo credit: EarthDayPictures via Visualhunt / CC BY

"We must cherish one another, watch over one another, comfort one another, and gain instruction that we may all sit down I heaven together."
(Lucy Mack Smith, 1775–1856)
https://www.goodreads.com/author/
quotes/77656.Lucy_Mack_Smith

14. <u>Law of Forgiveness – People hugging</u>

Photo credit: Unhindered by Talent via Visualhunt. com / CC BY-SA

"When you forgive, you in no way change the past – but you sure do change the future."
(Bernard Meltzer, 1916–1998)
https://www.brainyquote.com/quotes/
quotes/b/bernardmel132866.html
Ervin/Laws/210

15. <u>Law of Free Will or Law of Choice pg. 110 – Hanging rope bridge</u>

Photo credit: Kiwi Tom via Visual hunt / CC BY
"Behold, here is wisdom, and let every
man choose for himself."
(D&C 37:4)

16. <u>Law of Giving and Receiving – Small Water Falls</u>

Photo credit: Ian Sane via Visual Hunt / CC BY

"For it is in giving that we receive."
(Francis of Assisi, 1181–1226)
https://www.brainyquote.com/quotes/
quotes/f/francisofa121465.html

17. <u>Law of Gratitude – Praying hands</u>

**Photo credit: ^@^ina (Irina Patrascu Gheorghita)
via VisualHunt.com / CC BY**

"Cultivate the habit of being grateful for every
good thing that comes to you, and give thanks

continuously. And because all things have
contributed to your advancement, you
should include all things in your gratitude."
(Ralph Waldo Emerson, 1803–1882)
https://www.goodreads.com/quotes/14132-cultivate-
the-habit-of-being-grateful-for-every-good-thing

18. Law of Health - Exercise -

Photo via Visual hunt

"Let food be thy medicine and medicine by thy food."
(Hippocrates, 460–377 bc)
http://www.goodreads.com/quotes/62262-let-food-
be-thy-medicine-and-medicine-be-thy-food

19. Law of Increase – Bee on Flower

Photo credit: Me now0 via Visual Hunt / CC BY-ND

"I believe that God gives you hopes and dreams in a size
that's too large, so you have something to grow into."
(Lynn A. Robinson)

https://www.goodreads.com/quotes/715204-i-
believe-that-god-gives-you-hopes-and-dreams-in

20. Law of Justice – Hammer of Justice

Photo credit: toridawnrector via Visual hunt / CC BY-SA

"Every act, every deed of justice and mercy and benevolence, makes heavenly music in Heaven."

(Ellen G. White, 1827-1915)
https://www.brainyquote.com/quotes/
quotes/e/ellengwhi533158.html

21. Law of Knowledge and Wisdom – Pile of books

Photo credit: *S@ndrine Néel* **via** *VisualHunt* / *CC BY-ND*

Ervin/Laws/212

"Any fool can know. The point is to understand."
(Albert Einstein, 1879–1955)
http://www.goodreads.com/quotes/72361-any-
fool-can-know-the-point-is-to-understand

22. Law of Unconditional Love – Dog and cat

Photo credit: Yukari* via Visual Hunt / CC BY-SA

"Good works is giving to the poor and the helpless, but divine works is showing them their worth to the One who matters."

(Criss Jami)
https://www.goodreads.com/quotes/463980-good-works-is-giving-to-the-poor-and-the-helpless

23. Law of Obedience – Sky, Water

Photo credit: Beverly & Pack via Visual Hunt / CC BY

"Obedience brings success; exact obedience brings miracles."

(Russell M. Nelson)
https://www.lds.org/church/news/elder-nelson-delivers-spiritual-thanksgiving-feast-to-mtcs?lang=eng

24. Law of Patterns – Plant pattern

Photo credit: brewbooks via Visualhunt / CC BY-SA

Our character is basically a composite of our habits.
Because they are consistent, often unconcious patterns,
they constantly, daily, express our character.
(Stephen Covey, 1932–2012)
https://www.brainyquote.com/quotes/
quotes/s/stephencov132958.html

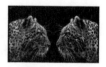

25. Law of Polarity – Red, blue tigers

Photo credit: reXraXon via Visualhunt.com / CC BY

"What good is the warmth of summer, without
the cold of winter to give it sweetness."
(John Steinbeck, 1902–1968)

https://www.goodreads.com/quotes/54619-what-good-
is-the-warmth-of-summer-without-the-cold— John
Steinbeck, Travels with Charley: In Search of America

26. Law of Sacrifice – Clock and Apple -

Photo credit: chefranden via Visual Hunt / CC BY

"It's not hard to decide what you want your life
to be about. What's hard, she said, is figuring
out what you're willing to give up in order
to do the things you really care about."
(Shauna Niequist)
— Shauna Niequist, Bittersweet: Thoughts on
Change, Grace, and Learning the Hard Way
https://www.goodreads.com/quotes/tag/sacrifice

End Summary - puzzle piece -

Photo credit: professor.jruiz via VisualHunt.com / CC BY
Your life is like a puzzle, and only God knows
what the end result will look like. Let him
put the pieces together. ~ Anonymous
https://www.dailyinspirationalquotes.in/2014/12/
your-life-is-like-a-puzzle-and-only-god-knows-
what-the-end-result-will-look-like-let-him-put-the-
pieces-together-anonymous-spiritual-quotes/

Law of Endurance

Enduring to the End-Start/Finish line -
Photo credit: Andrew_D_Hurley via
Visualhunt / CC BY-SA

Life is a series of experiences, each one of which makes
us bigger, even though sometimes it is hard to realize
this. For the world was built to develop character,
and we must learn that the setbacks and grieves
which we endure help us in our marching onward.
(Henry Ford, 1863–1947)
https://www.brainyquote.com/
quotes/keywords/endure.html

"This material is neither made, provided, approved, nor
endorsed by Intellectual Reserve, Inc. or The Church of
Jesus Christ of Latter-day Saints. Any content or opinions expressed, implied or included in or with the material
are solely those of the owner and not those of Intellectual
Reserve, Inc. or The Church of Jesus Christ of Latter-day
Saint."

Note: All attempts were made to contact the original
author for permission of their quote. For any that were not
found, I apologize but appreciate their words.

About the Author

Sonja is an Idaho farm girl that graduated from Brigham Young University–Idaho (Ricks) with an associates of art degree before moving on to Brigham Young University–Provo to receive her bachelor of art degree. After her children left the nest, she continued on to LDS Business College in Salt Lake City and received an associates in applied science in the field of interior design. With an interior design group, she had a very memorable time traveling through England, Scotland, France, and Spain. She has been a theater set designer for many years and has produced paintings for her family and friends. Sonja has the pleasure of teaching Gospel Doctrine in her Sandy ward. She has a great interest in Universal Laws and how they are used by God and man to produce great lives. She enjoys beautiful things, places, and music. She lives with her husband in Sandy, Utah. They have five children and six grandchildren.

CPSIA information can be obtained
at www.ICGtesting.com
Printed in the USA
BVOW11s0846300418
514822BV00002B/405/P